WATER STREET DAYS

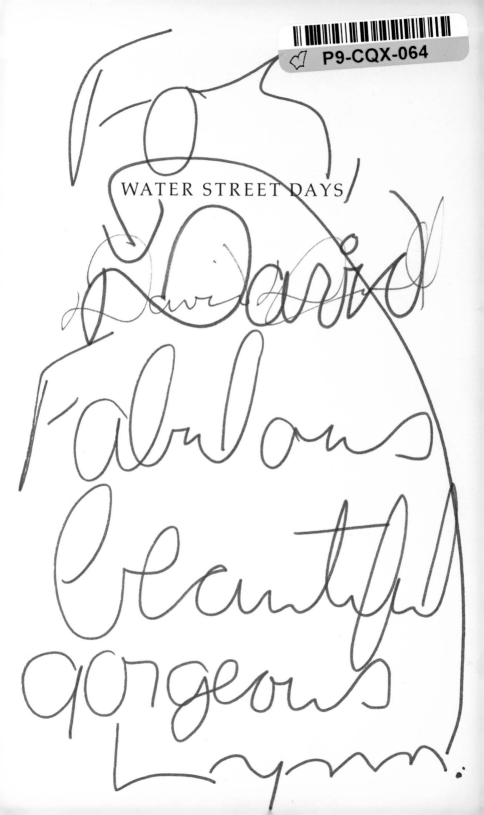

BOOKS BY DAVID DONNELL

POETRY

Poems 1961
The Blue Sky 1977
Dangerous Crossings 1980
Settlements 1983
The Natural History of Water 1986
Water Street Days 1989

FICTION

The Blue Ontario Hemingway Boat Race 1985

NON-FICTION

Hemingway in Toronto: A Post-Modern Tribute 1982

Water Street Days

POEMS AND STORIES

David Donnell

Canadian Cataloguing in Publication Data

Donnell, David, 1939–
   Water street days : poems and stories

ISBN 0-7710-2848-2

I. Title.

PS8557.O54W38 1989   C811".54   C89-093728-1
PR9199.3.D66W38 1989

The Publisher would like to thank the Ontario Arts Council for its
assistance.

Set in Aldus by The Typeworks, Vancouver

Printed and bound in Canada

McClelland & Stewart Inc.
The Canadian Publishers
481 University Avenue
Toronto, Ontario M5G 2E9

This book is for Nancy Kennedy

'This new interest was a valued novelty in whistling, which he had just acquired from a Negro, and he was suffering to practise it undisturbed. It consisted in a peculiar birdlike turn, a sort of liquid warble, produced by touching the tongue to the roof of the mouth at short intervals in the midst of the music. . . .'

Mark Twain
The Adventures of Tom Sawyer

'This is a pure story, whatever you may think.'

Julian Barnes
Flaubert's Parrot

'I don't like weakness, but I like to drink.'

Montgomery Clift
From Here to Eternity

CONTENTS

I

WATER STREET

I have to understand this about myself.
That I have been
raised on the family as if it were a form
of baseball.
Like a fielder, a tall gangling
straw-haired country boy, mouth full of butterflies,
big chin.
Call me Ontario Blueberry, if you like. Love

fumbles in the sun-bleached field of the family
& is never
entirely successful/ until it learns to judge the wind,
foresee a strategic bunt,
or calculate the effect of late rain on the grass.
Beliefs
are important. Even for the white grizzly bear chewing
his wad of Jebediah on the bench.
But the way you lurch
for a sharp grounder past 1st, or leap at the top of the wall
on a windy night, or slide into 3rd,
is how your
friends will know you
& talk about you after the game.

Rules in themselves, *en soi,* as the French philosophers say,

are a form of mercy that allows us to keep ourselves fit
for humdrum or excess or glory.

1

My father didn't spend very much free time
on the big ground floor of our house in St. Marys.
                                        A study
upstairs where he wrote fine Greek notes in the margins of books,
& a workroom. Fresh shavings, planes & levels, across the hall.

Sometimes he would sit outside in a wood & canvas lawn-chair
and read.
            To me at 4½ it must have seemed
as if he was walking through blue air in a Grimm myth,
                                                    or
sitting outside the Gare Centrale in Paris. Someone who was
very present but whom you could never speak to.
                                        Athletic,
comfortable. Neat
                in a well-cut grey tweed suit, glancing
at his watch occasionally, & flipping
pages,
        browsing through a new translation of Thucydides.

I would stretch out my tiny white hand to him
like a painted cream pitcher and he would stare through me,
looking ahead to supper, no doubt,
and my mother's delicious marrow soup.

Little things seemed to irk my father like a crack
in the universe. I remember a favourite
brace & bit,
a shotput, milkweed pods, a hammer left out in the rain
& a torn page from the M–O volume of the encyclopedia.

Of course, I got a great deal of affection from my mother.
                                                              Not
chocolate or toys, but animated conversations.

That was a problem with my father. We didn't talk.
I admired him. I thought he was handsome.

My father had a thick moustache,
but was otherwise as clean-shaven as a soldier in mufti.

We had a kind of truce. I avoided the study
& workroom areas to some degree.
                                      But wood shavings smell
fresh. Greek letters have beautiful shapes. Like islands. He
refrained from trying to teach me Greek at the age of 4,
                                                  which
was probably just as well. My father would throw his Grade 13
students across the room for missing conjugations in Latin.

My father was about to be told he had a heart condition.
I think he could feel this condition coming on.

He was quite often tired in the evening.
He stopped snowshoeing & lacrosse,
                                    games
he'd played effortlessly when he was at college.

Looking back, my father reminds me now
of the stoic mother and son in Arshile Gorky's famous painting,
Mother.
His own mother was Scottish and a talented painter.
Mary left James making photographs of the harbour in Mazatlan
when my father was 8.
I have a photograph of my father
at that age, standing in front of a sedate row house
in San Francisco.
It is 1912. Wilson is about to enter
the White House and make a mess of Versailles
with his Stutz Bearcat haircut.
America
is prosperous, but not given to mass publishing or free
tuition.
Back in Toronto, at college, medalist in rugby
& the 100 metres, his mother dies, 2 weeks before he graduates
at 21. Upstairs, he breaks the 2 chairs in his Knox study.

My father died, of a minor heart condition
after 30 years of teaching, when I was 9½.
The year
that Boston won the pennant. A silver steel shotput
lying out on the front lawn.
Glinting. Until the boy
in the painting
with his short hair & dark slash eyes,
walked out and lugged it into the front hallway.

Where it sat, like a bright gravity.

My father sits across the dining-room table from me, his neat oxford stripe shirtsleeves tucked up at the elbow with silver sleeve bands, gold signet ring winking in the early evening light. He is barely concealing his gargantuan impatience with me. It flickers around the corners of his mouth. The fury seems to move back and forth like a coal car rocking on steel ball-bearings somewhere in the dark middle of his head. His mouth is firm, his hazel eyes, which used to remind me of August flowers growing wild in the backyard of our friends the Rices' cottage, now seem almost dark blue-grey. He bends his great head over the steaming bowl of vegetable soup my mother has spent part of the afternoon preparing, while he has been teaching at the Collegiate, classics, history, and inhales briefly. Then he takes the giant ladle and dishes out a full bowl for himself, passes the tureen to my older sister; she is sitting across the table from me with her dark gaminish head cocked to one side, delicately chewing her thumb.

He proceeds to eat, precisely tilting the large spoon into his mouth without spilling a drop, and without schlurping. His hair is short and well-brushed. There is a touch of grey above the ears. His black ebony-handled brushes sit one beside the other on top of his bureau every morning when I walk past their master bedroom on the second floor to wash, brush my teeth, and run a comb through my hair. His hands are extremely clean, nails cut evenly and short like a surgeon's. His eyes are hazel one minute, then cool as ice. He doesn't look at me.

Sometimes I stop across from the St. Marys Ice-House on Main Street after school. I like to watch the men with their

8

quilted shoulder reinforcements, ice picks dangling like pistols or fish from their belts, loading the trucks for the last afternoon run. The ice smokes in the fresh butter-soft afternoon sunlight as the men load it into the trucks with tongs. My father doesn't smoke. He has never smoked. He was far too much of an A student and college athlete to get involved in pennant-waving, tobacco, or random parties with flasks of Canadian rye and model-A Ford roadsters. My father isn't strict, he's exact; not stern, merely correct and explosively forceful.

I sit with my large mouth open in trepidation above my untouched soup, although I am hungry, and wait for him to speak. He has no intention of speaking until my mother brings in the main course, sweet moist ham with mounds of fresh mashed potatoes and smart crisp green snap beans from the garden at the back of our house. The dog is out there. It is still light. There is a patch of sunlight on the dining-room windowsill. I will be allowed to go out and play after supper.

'Don't squirm; keep your head up, be calm.' I was told this as soon as I was allowed to eat dinner with my parents at the huge mahogany dining-room table. So I never do. I sit openmouthed in trepidation, but I'm very calm, hands plain as mushrooms on the table in front of me. Calm, I sit frozen. Thinking about my grandfather, Duncan. Duncan was superb and had died recently. I thought about Florida and Duncan a lot that summer.

Duncan was tall and rawboned and elegant, tanned and casual, ruminative, hands in pockets; odd things in pockets: Irish Twist tobacco, small bars wrapped with gold-foil seals with sharp stickers at the ends, which he used to give me to play with while he took out one of his favourite jackknives and pared off a small palmful of shavings for his pipe. I was seduced by those seals, those seals and the smell of tobacco. My mother says I am very much like my father: obsessed with exactness; but I am also very much like Duncan: fond of fishing, auction sales, and old prints.

9

The Spartan hoplites were like this: young boys with their shirts rolled up at the wrists, overturning cars in the streets, eating dark bread and honey with bowls of goat's milk, invading gymnasiums, illuminating the Collegiate in the middle of the night with electrical cords.

When he does speak, the silence is more terrible than clashing brass instruments. First, he puts down the soup spoon very precisely at the edge of his plate. Then he stares down the long mahogany length of the table as if his eyes were piercing straight through the south wall. The blood rushes into his face like rivers. His eyes flex. Then he tears off his tie, which was tucked into his shirt, rips open his shirt and roars: 'I want to buy something. I want to sell things I already own. I want to sell the Collegiate I teach in and buy 5 brand new Pierce-Arrows. I want to sell my family and buy a large granite library like the Widener Library at Harvard. I want to sell this house and buy a Mausoleum.'

My father is frothing at the mouth. His hair is disarranged. He pulls out a handful of hair and throws it in the soup tureen. His eyes crackle like electrical storms. His face is like the dark summer night sky on the 24th of May, in Haliburton where we go for vacations. His hands are like deranged picnic tables. His fly bursts. His cock emerges huge and wet as a wriggling fish.

I am embarrassed. My mother will get up and leave the room. My sister will comfort him. I stare into the faint steam of my soup. I see alphabets and continents and legions in the small white xs and ys, and the celery and carrots. I have been taught to think, to take values seriously; I have been taught to be calm. I say nothing.

I am frozen like winter light on the panes of a public building at night, with the overhead electrical lights left on. The cleaning staff mops the floors with their pails of steaming water. A man called Marconi is sending radio signals across a pond. A photograph of a Canadian called Alexander Graham Bell talks to a city in New York State over a black bakelite device called a telephone. I am rapt. I love my father but I am weighted with the importance of the values he has taught me. My intestines bleed but I say nothing. I sit quietly and stare past my sister's beautiful dark head out the open dining-room window at the garden.

'Bring me home something I can buy and sell, for Christ's sake,' he says to me. He has not taught at the Collegiate for several months. They discovered he has a heart condition when he went for his general checkup.

I say nothing. I resolve to bring home a pair of rubber-handled pliers, some wrenches, a medicine ball.

My mother gets up and leaves the room. She returns with a fresh napkin in her hand. Yellow flowers curl up at the corners of her mouth like a summer field. My sister smiles at her.

'We forgot to say grace before the soup,' my mother points out. She is gentle but formidable.

'Are we going to say grace?' says my sister. She giggles.

The summer air is as thick as pollen. My left shoulder is full of light. There are small bits of yellow flowers in the soup. My heart is like a football. I hear one of my father's students at the local Collegiate say something like, 'Throw me that pigskin. Go for it, babe.' I lower my head slowly over the cold soup and pray for letters the size of spaniels.

One of my mother's best stories, and she had several,
was about how my uncle Lorne, Duncan's
brother,
            would stand at the foot of her bed, in Galt,
and wave one plump forefinger at her.
                                He had plump fingers,
he was a plump man, if it comes to that,
in his dark blue 3-piece suits with the gold watch-chain.
                                He had a
plump baby face, did Lorne, a peeved baby, a petulant fella,
with his fine gold glasses on a dark cord;
                                but he had a nice
smile, all told,
and he would stand at the foot of her bed around 9 or 10
o'clock
        and he would wave that plump finger and say,
'O that Teddy Roosevelt, thaaat Teddy Roosevelt;
he goes to Africa and he shoots little baby elephants.'

            And my mother who was about 8 or 9 years old
at this time,
            would sit up in her bed, bolt upright
I imagine, electric as a blue heron

in her embroidered white nightgown with her black curls,
                                                she
had a mass of black curls at this age, say the photos,
which I didn't see when I was a child,
                                and it's amazing
how well those Kodaks last without any chemical fix,
                                            cascading,

effulgent all around her head like a halo of dark olives.

And my mother would say, 'No, he doesn't, no he doesn't,
he does not go to Africa and shoot little baby elephants.'

     He was being avuncular and sweet, but she was
electric in her defence
          because her father,
old sawbones Duncan,
the bit & drill dentist with the rakish eye,
admired Teddy Roosevelt the way boys admire French tubas.
                                     The
straight truth is that George Dewey blew the Spanish fleet
sky high out of Manila Bay in 1898;
                    true also
that Annie Oakley could put her head between her legs,
she never wore panties
under those fringed skirts, and shoot mirrors
at a hundred feet with a six-gun in each hand. There were
men in this period who
               massacred passenger pigeons
and stacked them on boxcars. Men who dropped
dead in the streets of New York from a pickaxe handle
across the mouth. Broke my mouf,
you fucker.
     Women who sold their bodies in garment lofts
as a way of getting half an hour, if it took that long,
away from the sewing machine.
          And women in velvet dresses
who endured cigar burns marching on suffragist demonstrations.

     But the apothecary's truth of this cockamamy
is that Teddy Roosevelt didn't shoot
very many elephants.
          He wasn't a very good marksman.

He was energetic. The man had the heart of an elephant,
with a striped hat on his head and his tweed trousers
hoisted over his calves for easy wading on the shore
of Oyster Bay. He once said, 'Walk softly and carry a big
stick.' Thinking no doubt of the recent troubles
in Europe with the French and the Germans. He wasn't
a very good shoot. I think he got 1 elephant,
or maybe 2.

The raiders slaughtered the passenger pigeons.
The raiders slaughtered the buffalo.

The Irish cop on the beat
put the pickaxe handle across the Italian's mouth.

TRUCKS

I didn't see my new stepfather around the house very much, but I got to know a completely different side of him out on the truck. I would go out with him quite often on Saturdays. Bill had been on a farm before he came to Galt. But after they were married, he bought second-hand furniture from around the county, and further, and sold it to various shops: bureaus, bedsteads, dining-room tables. Oak, white pine, dull cherrywood, bright bird's-eye maple.

There was a series of trucks. They were all ½-ton blue Ford pickups. It was the only colour of truck he liked. We had cars also. We had accidents with the cars sometimes. We had an accident with the Dodge, and we had one skidding on the ice on Grand Street with the Chev 4-door. I didn't drive. I was 10. 10 to 12. Big for my age. Bill drove. He was clever. He couldn't speak Latin or anything like that, but he was industrious and blithe, and he had his moments. We never had accidents with the trucks. One hand on a take-out coffee, left hand out the window, he could drive with his knees. It was a good trick.

Anyway, we would take the truck and range around the countryside. Some Saturdays, we might go all the way north to Goderich, to check out an old wardrobe; or west to London, and come back with a huge cast-iron bell from an abandoned church. The bell looked odd sitting on the back of the truck like a gigantic black bird, but there would be a buyer for it. Service stations, small-town lunchbars where we would stop for hamburgers, country hotels where I would be given a bacon & tomato sandwich; my stepfather would pour down a few quick draughts of Molson's or Labatt's, and we would be on our way.

15

The farms were often better than the houses in town. Up and down old gravel country roads, off through fields or wooded areas beyond the highway. It was amazing what some of these people had stored away. There was money in this practice. Bill was a shrewd buyer and a good talker. He was quite a soft-soaper, with or without suds. The farmers, sagacious but reticent, experts on crops and sick animals, would nod their heads and shrug, consider, shrug, and then sell for a bit more than his initial offer.

Saturdays of hot mornings, bright lazy afternoons, dark nights. Mostly in the summer, but sometimes in the winter. Lunchbars and small hotels I could never afterwards, I admit, remember the names of. Individual farms, churches, small towns with a population of maybe 250, containing a general store, 2 churches, and perhaps one great house set off by itself before suddenly the highway, always going somewhere always leading in and out of more and more of these small towns, would swallow you up again. Sometimes those were the best moments. The long quiet periods in between towns, with nothing but your bright headlights cutting through the soft dark; and then the almost delicious advent of another small town coming up.

Those trucks still tug at me as a symbol of highways and negotiations, of pulling into small farmyards at 9 in the morning, sloshing through mud on our way down to the barn with a farmer vaguely interested in selling an old brass bed he put away in the loft 2 or 3 years ago. Nights coming home late in the spring, rainy dark, windshield wipers consistent as clockwork, wiping and re-allowing visions of slow cars and trucks up ahead. The fields of childhood remain constant, the roads, the gumshoe boots and the equipment and old barns remain. The sky and the trees vary in my specific memories. But the truck is clear, opulent, as a way of moving among nature and people at the same time; of people in the fact of nature, and of art in the casual play of commerce.

We had problems at home sometimes, but he was OK on those Saturdays out in the country. He knew the towns and he knew something about furniture. Bill had a funny sense of humour, and there were always the C&W stations on the radio. They were pretty funny, too, sometimes. Songs about heartbreak and sawdust and ½-empty liquor bottles. He would whistle blithely. But the truck, the truck itself, empty in the morning and loaded at night, its mobility, and those roads, is what I missed most when I came to Toronto with its university and its great conservatory, città di luci, the city of lights.

DANCING AT THE RENOVATED KING EDWARD (VII)

1

                    My mother was a tall, confident woman
and she loved telling stories
                              in between cooking
and the Armstrong recordings she played for me as a child.
Her favourite stories were usually from the Ohio Tafts,
or White Plains, NY, and they were about achievement.
About our grand although not immediate relatives.
Grandfathers and great uncles.
Hugh Cant had been President of the Gore Insurance
in Galt when he was 35. A flag at half-mast when he died.
William Howard Taft had taken the top 3 political offices.
                                        The Woodwards
had owned coaches and dark horses. A matched pair. Charles

Sabin Taft had sat beside the Shiloh cannon President's bed
and Mrs. Lincoln had given him Abraham's cuff-links. She
had been beside herself with grief.

                    Sometimes she told these stories
while knitting, brown & green socks with orange toes;
or she told them, oatmeal or chicken with dumplings,
over supper.
                    My mother's stories had tangible
starting points. Juicy. They were simple,
told in a pleasant easy-going voice;
they were graceful, all right, and they resolved well.

My sister and I liked the stories about Sarah Frances
from the fabulously wealthy Washington family,

and Duncan who was obviously a world-beater & a *Ding an sich*.

The interest was tangible. But, despite the chicken
and whole-wheat bread, there were unfulfilled hungers.

Boys are quick sleek dogs and the hunger
                              fanned by disaster
was beautiful. The hunger had a sweet edge: an angular
jackknife whose blade had the dark sweetness of cucumber
pickles. Stored on dusty shelves beside the cellar lumber
room. Where my rabbits died by accident one spring.

There have always been a lot of hungers
in my life.
Well-fed & wan at 12, hungry & handsome
by 17. Adrift & askew & stubbornly romantic. Day-
dreamy & steamy.
That's me, stubbornly romantic,
a farm boy for the having.

Parents have a way of seducing us.
Often with love.

Pictures on the wall spoke to me. I felt I was destined to
face life, and death also,
casually and with a cavalier attitude. I would tweak
Death's sharp nose and go out on King Edward's ballroom floor
in Toronto
under the crystal chandeliers

and dance with life in a red dress
until the French champagne corks popped
and the few social columnists chewed their nails
and fainted under the white tables with their feet in the air.

These stories of my mother's were a clear sketch
in blue chalk,
without very much brown ink at the bottom for sewer gratings,
garages, dead grass or street curbs.

(They were not really stories they were anecdotes, aspects,
green aspics,
flour, isolated facts, peppercorns & nuggets of black walnut
that my mother told as a sort of graceful habit

walking from dining room to kitchen
or while sitting in the living room knitting socks.)

They were fairly factual, not plumb centre, but middling
true. Less like
                    a plumb-line
than like a plum.

Eat your applesauce, angel face, and don't talk so much. You'll
wake up City Hall.

I told good stories, but about Vermeer & Goya
& Miro. Time was like water and I swam in it.
                                    Jackknifed by grace
or butterflied in Simcoe blue. I snuffled it up
in my wide happy mouth and blew it out of my ears
like a seal pup.

Lolled on my back on living-room floors telling stories
about the dark myths of Scarlatti the younger, & John Coltrane
& Sonny Rollins.
                    Red Skelton jokes,
Cyd Charisse; Einstein's theory of the slow curve ball
that repeats itself without ever being caught.
                                    That slow
curve ball doesn't seem to have an abrupt past tense.
Shelves of books in a cheap cluttered apartment with a view
of the Eatons' coach house over on Lowther,
                                    raw eggs
for breakfast, efficient, and a slow morning writing new poems
I probably won't publish for months.
                                    It puts a strain on my
favourite stories about Vermeer. Proust was wealthy.
My rent's overdue and I'm short at the bank again. Almost
as short as that famous dwarf of Goya's.
                                    Duncan was very good
on situations like this. Especially after the experience
of losing all his money on those oranges in Florida.

My mother's death was an ice-cube in my red left ear. That
kid who used to like stories about the President
woke up with a wet eagle in the back of his mouth.

The refurbished Prince of Wales' hotel

isn't a stranger anymore. I have lunch there sometimes
& I was dancing there last week with my friend

the botanist,
but I can't say I've knocked out any social columnists lately.

I think of Duncan in an old straw hat
catching baby alligators the size of logs down on the beach
and putting them back in the blue water to swim. I pick up

the worn tweed jacket and leave by the stairs to catch
some late morning sunshine before lunch.

This is my
only author appearance. Sans fielder's glove. Sans
breaking ball. Now, reader, we can go back to the past.
Or is it?

TENNIS

               I have a colour photograph of myself at 9½
in the spring of 1950.
                      A wide-eyed boy with a brush-cut
& a blue tennis ball. Like a white yak
with a blue tennis ball in its mouth.

My mother's remarriage was a problem and I had no specific words
with which to discuss it.
                    Most of my words were monosyllabic.
Especially with that blue tennis ball in my mouth.

Bird and I took our CCMs to Kitchener-Waterloo and I had 2
hot dogs with sauerkraut at a lunch-counter on Steidtler Street.

You wouldn't expect a blue tennis ball to be so evocative.

Balls come off the wall at different angles. Even the wind
coming through the oak trees over on Robinson Street
can influence the slow spin or trajectory of a ball.

               Michael Aiken said my mother was married to a
drunk and I fought him out in the schoolyard. Carol Percival
                           wasn't there
but Lynn Morris was. Lynn Morris said, 'Hit him, David,
black his eyes.'
               I slipped and fell in a mud puddle. It would
have been all right if I hadn't slipped.
                       My best friend Des
Nesbitt said, 'Don't worry about it. You can set his bicycle
on fire some afternoon.'

I played a lot of tennis against school walls
that summer.
St. Andrew's School, stately, red brick.
Sometimes the balls were pink or lime green,
but I liked blue for its cool freshness,
and that's what you see
in the picture: a boy with his eyes narrowed to slits,
dark, observant,
& a blue tennis ball in his mouth.

You have to acquire discipline. You have to bear down
on the ball and aim for a specific brick.

I could never beat my sister's boyfriend
Graham. Bright, 17, with dirty fingernails
and a remarkable backhand.
But I could make the ball spin either way, or make it float
like a pigeon coming up from under the dark bridge
at Victoria & Grand.
Brett Steiner was one of my 3
best friends that summer. Brett had fantails.
2, both blue.
We used to throw them off his roof and watch them climb
in the blue air & disappear.
Brett called them
'Tom' & 'Sunny.' They would tuck their smart heads down,
hunch their shoulders and look like large tennis balls

but would open their wings at the last moment
before plummeting. Then they would lift up
and sail off over the trees like dusky blue & grey clouds.

My family is always leaping up in my mind
like coloured water,
                    especially the period in Galt before
I was 12, my athletic father with his clipped moustache,

my mother amazed after his death,
                                sometimes a clear photograph
of an uncle or a blue Ford truck,
a financial disturbance,
a late afternoon May dinner under a big maple tree
at the side of our spacious house,
                            or a picture
of Kevin Menzies running across the huge side yard
carrying a fat toad & yelling 'Geronimo.'

        Now they are bringing the long picnic table
out to the front lawn.
                    My sister is reading
in her upstairs bedroom with a plate of sliced potato
& carrots beside her on the pine desk.

I walk around and watch what these people are doing.

My chemistry set is upstairs in the attic
with my microscope & a black notebook.
                                I'm probably
more interested in baseball right now.

My father muses perplexedly at the shoes of S.A. Wilson
who is taking his photograph.

Now they are bringing out the large red jugs
of lemonade and coffee.
My father was a Classics specialist
and died of a torn heart when I was 9½.

My mother and my stepfather were coming home one evening.
Bill was a little drunk.
They ran into a tree near the front porch of Sid Lapp's house
on Victoria.
I heard about this in detail
the next day at school.

My sister won a stack of scholarships and went off to college.

I dreamed of leaving home and living with friends who had a
pet kangaroo.

Galt in the early 50s.
This is where the Aladdin Cleaners truck slid out on the blue ice.
Where I first saw Carolyn Demeroff's new breasts.
Casual
scenes and a few disasters. A dining room,
the blue Ford
truck, the large yellow kitchen, a bright scene
as in the chickens we kept one summer
or the burning garage. Or occasionally
something as particular and simple
as a piece of blue burlap from Michigan, a certain shade
of mustard yellow brick, or a copy of one of my father's books.
The Brushwood Boy, for example.
Gorgeous colour plates.
I don't think I can remember reading it.

My mother was married twice. She lived
in a lot of different houses,
but she was always in love with her father — the lean, handsome
dentist, suntanned pundit & wit, Bojangles Cant.

She probably laid the dust on this love with a bucket
of cool water when she was 20. Became tall,
gracious & self-possessed. A young womanhood of satin dresses,
elm leaves,
Victrola 78s of Louis Armstrong playing *Darktown Strutters' Ball*.
Then she married at 26 and began to raise a beautiful family.

My athletic father died of Mitral Stenosis when I was 9½.
A mysterious tear
in the heart. My mother caused a small scandal in Galt. She
married an illiterate flim-flam man. He was Irish.
His name was Bill and he babbled stories about a place called
Chinatown. It was east of Waterloo County. They had card games
there. But he could
never hold a steady job.
                            Sweet William wasn't any substitute
for my father or Duncan. He cracked wise
like Bojangles, upbeat,
I guess,
and he had a kind of cheerful irreverence about his person.
Snap-brim fedora, lewd winks, finger drumming.

●

Duncan came back from Florida after 3
frosts in a row,

                    bruised oranges,
by way of Quebec,
broke, not bent, tall, brown, witty, irreverent,
& took a night-watchman's job at Massey-Harris in Galt.

Duncan who never picked her up out of her black
patent leather shoes when she was home from boarding school
on weekends.
                    Although he came & stayed with us in St. Marys
for several months.
Filled the hallway at 92 Wellington with rum tobacco,
risqué comments, & stories that made me think of soft green
water slapping the Florida piers in January.

I can remember crying when he died. Child's disbelief. It's
a terrible thing to be a child watching your mother
lose her father.
                    It can give you the impression
there isn't very much stability in the world.
                                        My mother
cried also. She told me the first time she cried over Duncan
was when she was 16. He was generous and as single-minded
as an elephant.

But she liked keeping Duncan's memory alive
in a box of old family silver,
an 1890s pocket-watch, a photograph
of Duncan sitting out on the wide back White Plains sunporch
in shirtsleeves with his bourbon and the 2 dogs.

                            ●

        My beautiful mother
was in this respect like a homing pigeon. A wild-eyed horse.
A plunging red kite.

Sweet William drank. The mortgage
was never paid on time. The furnace blew out. The furniture
had to be sold.

But the obvious didn't occur to me until many years later.
That Plain Bill reminded my mother of Duncan,
the snappiness, peppery,
cheerful
I guess you would call it

although I rode around with him in the truck enough times.

So, for her, he was funny sunny Bojangles Cant. White
shirtsleeves. Crinkly around the eyes.
Husband of the beautiful woman
who died when my mother was 2 weeks old.

                                   Life is strange.
                                   And then she was
playing hopscotch out on the front walk. One, two,
buckle your shoe, three, four, shut the door.

Duncan could snap his fingers in the sunny afternoon room
and make a circus appear.
                      But fathers
live in Siam, or Florida, or Minsk.

There was a passion for Duncan, and an empty field
with some crows up in the ash trees.

        The crows said, Duncan.

ROWING

It is 6:45 a.m. Early sunrise. No birds. Cedars & Lebanon.

The 2nd piece of chocolate softens and spreads into a dark pool
on my tongue
                    and this image comes to me for no apparent
reason,
            of 3 people in a large boat
like the rowboat in Van Gogh's *The Bridge at Arles.*

Granted, I cannot be sure of the identity of the man rowing,
                                            white jacket,
                                            dark moustache,
but one of the women is my mother at 26, shortly after her
marriage to my father.
                        It is a clear day. My mother is very
young and she is wearing a long-sleeved white blouse
open at her neck for the sun,
and is trailing her hand in the blue water.

            This is on Lake Ontario and it is in 1930
when Buffalo was still a beautiful city.
(Canadian is a good name for a railway, but southwestern Ontario
is a country.) This is one of our lakes, in addition to
                                Huron & Erie.
They had concerts in those days. They had concerts in parks.
And fireworks out on the lakes. The great orange brass
of the French horns, & the tuba
which I always think of as distinctively American although
it isn't,
        thumpa thump, German, ist Deutsch.

●

Sunnyside Beach, if you can call it a beach,
sandy, seagull-dotted,
                                        like a spit. Parked cars, thick August
humidity. People sleeping on blankets spread out on the dark
grass. Florence in a print dress and her itinerant husband.
Girls and boys wading at night in black inner tubes.

Cool, blue, pretty, 53 miles across. (Ned Hanlan was a great
sculler. Middle-class boy. Advantages. Handsome. Clean-
                                                    shaven.
Medals & whisky. Canadian sunshine. Ned was a great sculler.

I think of him often sitting out on the Point in a canvas
lawn-chair drinking the whisky from a large glass.)

Sunnyside Beach and the Scarborough Bluffs – there is a rough,
black slate colour to this spontaneous image induced by
chocolate,
                    not chocolate itself
but more the colour of fat slugs, or the wet underside
of some old maple logs after a spring rain.

Somebody should write a book about all the different
lovers who have walked along Sunnyside Beach at midnight.
You could have a chapter on the 20s, the 30s,
but always lovers, and always at midnight.

Chocolate mud. Silt. A gold ring. The metal top of a soda
pop can, Verner's, circular, 1983.

●

                    I am wearing jeans this morning, barefoot,
2nd-hand Milan shirt.

That lake. Blue. As in the blue copper sulphates I used to
play with in the attic lab as a child.

How can I put one photograph over the other as a technician
                                                    would do
very simply with a colour transparency and a light-board?

The terrible part of this image,
that makes me crumple the blue & red glossy paper
until my hand bleeds, is the darkness,
                              black slate,
that comes over me as I sit motionless at the kitchen table.

Old images coming up to the surface and gashing on rocks.

Dark out this morning. Spring. Moody rain, mineral
traces of urine, gas, ammonias & slag.

Bright sunlight.
                    The lake is gigantic and beautiful
in summer. My mother's favourite dog
was a red chow. Her favourite fruit was Niagara peaches.
She was extremely fond of chocolate.

(Smelting acids, plastic compounds & detergent wastes.)
Blue, wet.
                    My father was never self-indulgent.
He was athletic and had hands the size of oarlocks,
but a late-night Lake hawk tore out his heart.

            Ned Hanlan is a myth that will live forever.

1

My mother was fairly social before marriage.
Not extravagant, just social. My father had a lot of warm
and domestic attitudes, although he was an athlete
and a scholar. He bought flowers, for example,
but never took her to sports events even if he was playing,
or dancing in Hamilton.
                            But after the first child
appeared, my sister Nancy,
                            Arnold developed a great calm
passion for his woodworking shop on the second floor of #92,

and for his study directly across the hall
from his lathes & planes.
                            So there were small piles of clean
wood shavings on one side, and neat blue fountain-pen
notes in the margins of open textbooks across the way.

This was fine. My mother plunged
into the adventure of children, one of a number of activities
she was especially good at,
                    gifted,
a natural & gracious talent, as in a natural vitality,
all the little steps, baths, teaching us to read.
                              The house
shone as if it were on display. I can remember reading
about the princess with the 3 gold apples,
                         the Greek guy
who ate an entire trough, and, when I was 6, Fenimore
Cooper's *The Deerslayer*, with colour tip-ins.
                              She was an
extremely beautiful woman with a faultless manner. They
used to sit at opposite ends of the big living-room sofa
with their feet touching
and read Dickens & newspapers & D.H. Lawrence.

But around the time Nancy and I were 11 and 17,
things changed.
They had started out as 2 separate people
overlapping,
communicating, their stockinged feet touching.
Then there were pauses. Pauses are metaphors. Like the Grand,
which used to flood each spring, lapping against a boat dock.
Now they became separate houses on opposite sides of the river.

My mother had her second marriage which involved
lunchbars,
used cars, the occasional movie. My father read
a great deal. Moderns.
He let his moustache grow thick as a pine cone. He was tired

of the Greeks. Even of the one he told me had invented
the telescope to look at boats from a great distance.
We never discussed these novels, cf. textbooks & lathes.
He let his moustache grow as thick as a shoebrush. I was 11.
He read a great deal. Huxley, Wodehouse, Chesterton,
Hemingway, Lawrence & Ford.
My sister who got 95% in Greek
& 97% in Latin wore lipstick and had a boyfriend
who took her to baseball games. Her girlfriend was in love
with Sandy Forrester. He was 18 and had a motorcycle.

There were a lot of novels around in the front living room
of 2 John Street. My father read & enjoyed them.

4

My sister and I stayed with our mother,
but I visited back and forth.
There were a lot of novels around
in the front room of 2 John Street. My mother and Bill
used to sit around the kitchen table a great deal
on the east side of the river
and talk about nothing.
But they did this with a sort of humour and pleasure.

Sometimes he would get drunk on Friday nights
and then there was turbulence. They went to movies on weekends.
It wasn't that bad. I would think
about this coming back across the river, crossing the bridge
with the pigeons ducking & billing underneath,
that my father
despite his prowess hadn't taught me to throw a good curve,
or to pass the football and make it float
as Pindar, the great Greek poet whom my father admired,
might have described it –
twirling through blue air
like a perfect spiralling horizontal of the sun.

That became my resolve as a child;
not to throw long ones up the side the way my friend Looney's
lanky older brother could do,
but to be able to describe these things.

Description is power. A form of power. My father could read
like a railway engine devouring coal, and he could generalize,
true,
but he could not describe.
Description is tangible.

Language is a going clear. Being able to put things into words
is a form of love, like the long pass up the sidelines,
or those dark pigeons
                    ducking & billing under the Grand Bridge.

HILLS

They aren't steep granite rises, or cliffs,
or mountain slopes. ,
They are simply hills.
Like the hills you see in the average
small town, or sometimes between 2 farms.

But coming into Toronto by car what you notice most
is the bridges, and after bridges, the overpasses and ramps.
Yonge Street Hill, for example, rises up from Lake Ontario
as gradually as a child's step in some blue water.
There are parks, even a zoo, but you have to consult a map.
The subways are fast.
Hills don't have elevators.
The city planners in Toronto don't know how to clean a bluff.
Wards don't have hills.
Some of the Indians
who used to live here made burial mounds. Other Indian tribes
used to put their dead in trees.
Soldiers traditionally leave hearts scrawled on rough cement
with 'Bad Harold was here.'

I associate hills with bicycles, and childhood with my mother.

OK, these hills in my case
were personal and casual.
We lived on Wellington Street Hill
in St. Marys, above Trout Creek,
the cement works & Main Street; below the Victorian granite
high school where my father taught Classics
to indifferent clean-cut seniors.

After that, there was John Street Hill
in Galt, 2 John Street,
                    just off a small gravel path
and a grassy incline that sloped down to the Kenneth Hay Knife
Co. Ltd.
            We lived next door to St. Andrew's School
where I fought Alvin Peters for saying my father didn't work
for a living. My father was in bed with a heart condition,
Mitral Stenosis; Alvin's father was a welder at Galt Brass
and brought home 40 packages of bacon twice a week.

            My father died. That was a gorge,
and then a hill.
We packed, eventually. We came to Toronto like rough oatmeal
& hog-fat Scottish immigrants getting off the CPR coach
at Union Station, and later bringing our possessions here,
suitcases and cartons in the back of a Ford roadster.

I loved Toronto so much, right off the bat,
because I thought it was the city, New York or Washington,
my mother had described to me when I was a child.
Small difference, I was entranced.
I liked the infinite streets and buildings like toffee.
I could have put the Hindenburg in my back pocket
and forgotten about it.
But those hills have a way of recurring, even in a lush
and sprawling city on a Lake.

            I used to have falling dreams as a child.
Now I have dreams about groups of people,
friends I don't see as often as I'd like to,
industrial offices, buses, trains, filing folders & postcards.

Archetypes can deflect and redevelop themselves just like fey
Sigmund's theory of sublimation: the man with the glass jars

in his living room, a blonde Hungarian woman
who thinks of horses and gets wet between the legs
when she wears rough cotton slacks,
men who feel effeminate when they wear sandals,
women who are afraid of birds, the boy who used to put a dish
of eggs between his legs, sit his cock in the dish, & beat
the eggs with an egg-beater.
Hills.

There are so many different kinds of hills.
The distance between myself and Patty Walthrop
sitting in the College Cinema.
Stuff that you see in newsreels.
The day I broke Bobby Sharpin's glasses.
Pork Chop Hill, Old Baldy, Heartbreak Ridge, Big Lonely.
It makes my heart bleed just to think of them.
Hamilton Mountain, the Laurentians, Vermont,
& the Catskills make me think more of driving than of skiing.

The hills in my case were simple.
Walking upstairs to sleep after kissing your mother goodnight
is a kind of hill. That tryst on the second-floor landing
with your sister, looking out at the moon, is a kind of hill.
We approach grass & stone and the hills determine us.
They leave an impression like bitter strawberries
eaten on midnight raids.

The part I liked best about walking or bicycling
up the hills
was the moment at or after the top,
when you walk
in the kitchen door and the kitchen is yellow & full of light.
Your father is dead and your mother is there.
She has a print
apron on and lets you smell the chicken steaming on the stove.

She gives you a glass of milk & some oatmeal cookies.
Oatmeal are the healthiest. I drink the tall white glass
of milk in gulps and have 3 cookies.
The dog whines. We have the largest dog in Galt. It is not
a hound. I like hounds best because of the way they run.
They run the way I run when I race across the schoolyard
with my head up jacket flapping & my arms loose.
I finish the glass of milk and go upstairs
leaving my books on the landing, and lose myself totally
in the instructions page for a Cessna airplane. Balsa
wood, airplane glue, blue & yellow paint.

Planes can fly above storms or take pictures from the air.

But even at the best or the worst of times it was the sweet
smell of steaming chicken,
the way light bounced off a yellow wall,

that made the frozen hills & the pedalling up almost a lark.

SWEET WILLIAM

My crazy stepfather had a fantastic
drunken confidence – for tilting back on a kitchen chair
dead drunk & liquid-eyed with 45¢ in his pocket,
who had nothing except a pink panda bear from the CNE,
pieces of string for cuff-links, a dark mouth screaming lugubrious
condemnations at the top of his lungs:

at the grey kitchen ceiling
or the invisible moon,
or the police who had not been called after all
or the guy next door who had just bought a new truck
or the drunk father he never met
or the mother he couldn't remember
or the 4 banks downtown who wouldn't cash his bad cheques
or the scrap-metal weighing-scales operator
who caught him splashing water on a goose-feather mattress
or the waitress who didn't like his 5¢ tip
or the farmers from whom he bought junk thresher-points
or the pigs who died after he invested his 100 dollars
or Sandy Sleighters who arrested him for drunk driving.

All these unfairly privileged figures of success
throwing his suitcases out the window
the cigarette case my mother gave him into the garbage
or my sister's boyfriend working at a summer job
the fat Ukrainian woman who sold him the strawberries for 75¢
or the kid at the garage who called him an asshole.

It was a gesture, the way another man might beat a forefinger
against his chest, or shove his thumb straight up in the dark
night air.

He would scream these fat words at the kitchen ceiling,
the moon that he couldn't see,
my dead Scottish father's picture,
my mother
who was pleading with him not to commit suicide.
The chair was a prop. The dozen beers were a prop.
And the broken plate the broken plate was also a prop.

        But he would reappear again by supper
of the following day,
having slept for about 16 hours,
                      friendlier, laughing,
clean-shaven, a fresh shirt,
the truck engine broken, a bawling out from the judge,
and he would balance all this desperation,
the failed truck business,
the NSF cheques,
his torn shoes,
the lost licence,
scrap metal & grapefruit rinds,
by spending every nickel in the house
on thick sirloins, fresh onions, peanuts, olives,
pretzels and deep-dish apple pies with chocolate ice-cream.

Then he would be off again on another attempt,
                          another
truck venture, a bank loan, a livestock purchase.

These unfairly privileged figures of success
lacked his abundant vitality.
Sandy Sleighters, Shmael Cooper, George Wong, Nellie Cavers.
Laughing   in the warm yellow kitchen
at 10 o'clock in the morning.
Clearing his throat like an opera singer with a broken nose.
Sweet William had a lot of confidence even when sober & broke.

It was always tomorrow or at the most a few days.
While the poplars along the school drive next door swayed
oblivious in the cool night air, the strawberries fattened,
the Galt Towel Co. laid off 30 more workers,
the furnace blew out, mortgage payments were due.

I turned 12.
My mother trimmed her dark hair.
After a few years we sold the house and moved to Toronto.

My stepfather walked into the St. Clair pool-room I was playing in one Saturday afternoon when I was 14. He looked around the big seedy room like a surprised farmer. Then he walked over to our table at the front by the cash register.

'Hello, Buck,' he said, with that stupid not-quite-right kind of breeziness he always affected.

That was a nickname he'd hung on me for no particular reason. Buck's was a service station with a knockout candy counter in the front back in Galt. Buck himself was a big fat older guy who owned the station; that is, he owned something, and he was about 450 pounds if he was an ounce.

I said hello, a little nonplussed, realizing vaguely that he'd said something over breakfast, in the bleak 4-room flat we were living in on Delaware at the time, about where was I going to be in the afternoon. He wanted to take the truck out to some farmer's in Pickering to look at some scrap farm machinery. I was out of high school but I didn't have a job. I was too intellectual for high school. They hadn't shown any interest in my efforts at commercial art. The English courses were juvenile. Plus I had a disobedience problem. Our living conditions at the time weren't motivating me very much. The poolroom, any poolroom, was a good territory in between high school intimacy and the work force.

'You're playing a game,' he said. I said yes. It was fairly obvious. I was playing with my friend Eddy. Eddy was 18 and had a part-time job. We were playing for 50¢ and Eddy, who was spotting me 10 points, a fair spot, was just about to break his cue because he'd missed a really easy shot on the brown ball. He'd done this just as my stepfather came in. The brown ball, worth 4 points, was from 2 feet, and it was right on the spot, just sitting there in the 'D,' like a neat brown pigeon waiting to go in the pocket.

'Too much juice,' Eddy said. Then he said he had to make a phone call.

'Here, you play with Dave,' he said, 'I'll be back in a minute. Don't miss any easy ones.' Then the dope went off to phone his girlfriend and there I was with my stepfather in this Italian poolroom on west St. Clair. I expected him to rip the table or miss the object ball completely. It was dumb. I tried a long shot on a red in the end and missed, but left the shooter uptable around the pink spot.

'Where's the fishing pole?' he asked some guy at the next table. The fishing pole. I thought he was having one of his morphine-and-beer-induced fits. It turned out he meant the long rake, a device for taking aim when the shooter is out of reach. There is also a short rake for when the shooter is only slightly out of reach or along the rail. You have to be a very good player, someone like Hatch or Bobby Simpson, to make difficult shots or fine cuts with the rakes. The long rakes tend to be wobbly. Obviously your perspective changes when you start sighting down a 7-foot pole.

The next second there he is just like a big tadpole. He's jumped up on the table like a regular player, like Bobby Simpson or somebody, resting on one elbow, and he's sighting down the short rake trying to bang one in the end. Then he jumps off the table, brushing some blue chalk dust off his old pants. He was dressed for the truck.

The truck was his total obsession, a blue Ford pickup; and when he finally sold or lost that truck, I forget which, then it was another truck and another truck or an old car. Dreams of trucks. He used the trucks, when he was lucky enough to have one, to squirrel around out in the countryside picking up scrap,

47

sheet metal, baling wire, old batteries, broken plough points, cast-iron implements.

He brought home an old bell once, it must have weighed close to 300 lbs. I couldn't budge the sucker.

'Well,' he says, 'I missed that one.' I was surprised at his foolish assurance. I didn't know the slug had ever played a game before, but I guess he must have. At least he knew how to hold his cue, more or less; a little sloppy, but not bad for an old guy, an old cracker, or however I thought of him. And he knew the hip name for the long rake.

The history of the long rake is probably more interesting than my late stepfather or his trucks. The long rake isn't really very much like a fishing pole. My grandfather gave me a great fishing pole for my 6th birthday. I can still see it in my mind's eye when I stop to think about it. It was about 6 or 7 feet long, bamboo, with a stop-catch reel that sang like a morning bird. They put it under the maple tree outside my bedroom window at the Wellington Hill house in St. Marys. St. Marys was before Galt. Toronto is anywhere. That was a fishing pole. Duncan, my grandfather, and I went fishing in Trout Creek and I think I caught 2 or 3 small bass, nothing to write home about.

My stepfather is a different mnemonic. I think of him and I think of his eyes bulging when he used to have fits. Or late at night when he used to sit at the kitchen table in Galt and stuff handfuls of bread in his mouth and wash them down with cold tea, squeezing the bag. I think of him up on the pool table that day before Eddy came back from phoning his girlfriend, and I realize now I think of him as a fish. Even though fishing pole isn't a good term for the long rake. Jesus turned Hell over with a harrow. He didn't use a rake. Harrow is the name of a very good English private school. They call them publics. I used to read *Stalky & Co.* by Rudyard Kipling for tips on how to build smoking lodges out in the woods. But after we came to Toronto I didn't have any real need for a smoking lodge. There were parks, main streets, alleyways, poolrooms, bowling alleys and vacant lots.

He didn't make any especially good or bad shots. But I think I resented him playing at all, or even being there. It was bad enough that he was married to my mother. He didn't have to show up at this poolroom that was at least 40 blocks from where we lived. But he didn't make any shots, and Eddy came back in a couple of minutes and said, 'This has to be the last game. She wants to go shopping.' I went out on the truck with crackpot for the afternoon. There was an old thresher, but the farmer wanted too much for it.

Thinking about my stepfather the other day, I thought of how hopeless he was; something made me think of the expression 'sick banana.' I'm not sure, but I think that's a '20s flapper expression. A period during which my mother wore lipstick occasionally.

A photograph made me think of the night he burned my sister's prom dress, rose, with organza at the bodice; an upcoming date with a friend to play pool made me think of the Saturday afternoon he dropped into the poolroom where I was playing, transgressing my sacred territory, sloppy, stupid-looking, although the other guys may have seen him differently. I saw myself, yesterday, walking across the kitchen to get a quart of milk out of the fridge, picking up that beautiful fresh 7-foot bamboo rod that Duncan gave me for my 6th birthday and casting for my stepfather way out in the grey April lake of southwestern Ontario: hooking the sucker like an old boot full of worms, an old hat full of shit, and wearily – the way it says in the Bible that 'They shall be tillers of soil and fishers of water' – wearily, Eddy, my old friend, the stop-catch singing like an early crow, reeling wild Billy in to the clarity of the sandy early-morning Toronto shore.

49

Chocolate is a natural substance
but so are the bananas that wind up in milkshakes, or the oats
that turn up in wholewheat & oat bread.
                                        Chocolate
was discovered by the Aztecs circa A.D. 850. Chocolatl.
Canadians used to believe that all chocolate was classical
and that it was a natural reward for children.
Hershey is OK, sometimes even with nuts.
                                        The dark room
in the cellar or is it the attic?
Chocolate is beautiful & clear & pure. True.
                                        But there are
chocolate factories in Michigan where they mix the crushed
chocolate paste with sugar, milk solids, cornstarch,
vegetable oil and other ingredients.

You could lose your house by becoming oblivious from chocolate.
A Galt house, a Toronto house.
You could lose your shirt.

Chocolate is one of those transcendental elements that can only
be understood by children, and people with contemplative minds.

            My great-grandmother Christie though. She never
ate chocolate. A radiant, beautiful woman. Built like a horse.
Stocky. She did nothing but work every day of her life until

she dropped in the fields outside of Ayr
pregnant with 12th child, love, sweet yellow stringbeans,
Jesus, chickens & fence posts. Dead as a cart horse
hit by a sledge-hammer.

                    ●

These are family stories that come down to you from your parents
about their parents. There might be a note of sorts,
Barthes would call it a sub-text; I would call it a bright wrapper.
Thinking more of a patchwork quilt or a Japanese kimono
than a Burnt Almond wrapper or an Eat-More.

But O fuck, John Cerutti, those Crispy Crunches.
They don't taste bad.
Those old Reese's peanut butter chocolate cups.

You should always keep a chocolate bar
in your desk drawer at work, your coat pocket
or the glove compartment of the car.
Chocolate is also good
for basketball. It gives you a positive rush before you go out
on the floor.
But don't get to the point
where you start stockpiling chocolate bars beside a
comfortable living-room couch. And waking up in the middle
of the night to eat half a Mars bar with a few gulps
of Ruby Rouge.
(That cheap Niagara wine will burn your stomach out, no matter
what the tourist promotion bulletins say.)
Don't drift
away from me like a phoney sunset
in one of those Deanna Durbin movies until I go crazy,
like the cat when they put
Keene's mustard up its asshole,
because I can't find you in the next room
with a copy of Christie's picture (big dark milky b&w photo-
gravure) on the wall behind you.

●

51

Chocolate is good for basketball
because it gives you a positive rush before you explode
onto the court.
                    Those milk solids, sugars, oils
& crushed nuts make the net basket stand out as if illuminated
by light & cigar smoke.
                         But you could lose your arm
by becoming oblivious from chocolate.
You could lose your mind, chum, or become reclusive.

You should have a little chocolate with your cornflakes
every morning. Before you crack that brown egg into a pool
of yellow butter.
                    Chocolate should make you feel loved
and reassured. Coffee houses and shopping plazas
have to come together in a balance.

I can shoot from the middle of the court,
& I can check with my hip protecting the ball,

I can do the sky hook,
& the Watusi Shuffle with my eyes half-closed,

chocolate, chocolate, chocolatta,

but down in the heartland I'm really a boy who loves cornfields,
justice, & hot dogs with mustard.
                         I don't want to wake up
tomorrow with nothing in my hands
except half a dozen bright crumpled empty wrappers
and a crumb of chocolate under my fat pink tongue.

MY SISTER PICKING RASPBERRIES

There was a green pickup truck the summer
my sister was 17,
                  and my sister would get up early for breakfast
and go to meet the truck across from the Dairy Bar
on Cedar Street
              where Peter & I always went on Sundays
for milkshakes, bought with whatever was left over
from our Saturday afternoon film.
                              We were younger, scuffed,
smart alecs. But I envied Nancy a bit, subtly,
because picking raspberries sounded like more fun
than playing tennis against the school wall,
or catching pigeons, or getting 97% in history.

This truck would take my sister and her friends
out to a farm near Woodstock,
                          and they would work long hours
(you pick raspberries in a stoop under a big straw hat
so you don't get sunburned) with a break for lunch
sitting around a long picnic table
eating my mother's sandwiches & devilled eggs.
                                          I think
she was paid $1.25 a bucket for the raspberries,
                                        but a girl
has to be careful: pick steadily, natch, plant after plant,
and exclude the soft red bruised berries,
& the hard little green ones that are bitter in your mouth
like wintergreen.
                And don't walk into the bushes
if you can help it. We're slim teenagers, eh, we're not
truckers.

I've thought of that summer several times
since Galt, and I always see my sister, in this particular scene
at least,
in a loose shirt & that big straw hat

that keeps you from getting sunburned while you make
an extra few hundred dollars toward 1st-year Classics & French.

Picking berries, thousands of tiny red raspberries
and sometimes the raspberry leaves or a delicate stem. I see her

through a soft reddish haze, the brown dirt smudged on blue
jeans and bare knees
made sweet with the smell of raspberries.

That was July,
and the blue-cuffed white gloves she wore for picking
lay around the house for a year or so after she went to college,
the black chow puppy Dusty wandered off to the country
one day,
my stepfather got drunk and smashed a kitchen window,
Chris Bickers began going out with Carolyn Demeroff,
there was a record snowfall in January.

I remember the gloves best when I think of this.
Better than
the truck or the farm which I visited once. Smudged brown,
torn,
I see them through a reddish haze lying by themselves
on a maple storage hutch, out in the pantry where we used to get
apples for breakfast.

ANECDOTAL

I was an extremely aggressive child. I used to bring home almost anything I found that I thought might be useful. This ran the gamut from a rugby ball or electrician's wrench to part of a telephone pole.

Mary Cavers and James Warren walking down by the harbour in San Francisco fell in love because they were both artists.

My father was extremely exact about money. If he was having dinner in a restaurant, or buying a shirt or even a newspaper, he liked handing over the exact change.

The Grand River used to flood the cellar of my uncle Lorne's pharmacy every spring.

2 of my father's best friends were the Hoggs. Frank Hogg & Helen Hogg. They were famous astronomers.

The RCMP stopped Duncan on his way back from Quebec once because of the square wooden 12 x 12 butterboxes on the back of his truck. They thought he had bootleg butter. The boxes were full of books.

My great grandmother's family had a matched pair of horses and a fashionable coach. We had a black DeSoto and it never went over 50 m.p.h.

I had a mass of dark curls as a child & this infuriated my father. They were cut before I started school. My Grade 1 picture makes me look like a sceptical POW.

She said the man who designed the logo for the Sherwin-Williams
Co.,
the logo that shows a tin of paint balanced on top of a globe
                                          and spilling over,
was the cousin of a friend she had gone to school with in Galt.

I felt an identification with this story.
                                    There was chicken
for supper and we were going to have potatoes with it instead
of dumplings.
                  She put carrots & parsley in with the chicken.
I was peeling & slicing the potatoes,
                                          after doing some painting.
The man had been an employee of Sherwin-Williams in Woodstock
or Paris.
              He had designed the logo in his spare time, at his
desk on a coffee or lunch break, and contributed it to the company.
She said they had never rewarded him for the image. They had
just thanked him.
                  He probably died poor, but the image
was out there on those tins of paint on the shelves
of thousands of different hardware stores all over the world.

          The Sherwin-Williams paint tin spilling
all over the world is an obvious symbol of ebullience.
Perhaps it's more American than Bill Davis or Bobby Orr.
Or perhaps the designer picked it up from a box
of Empire Cigars.
I have no idea of the nationality of the company,

but a Canadian designed this image or logo
and according to her story did not get paid.

We have so much food in Canada
and so many universities, that we have almost no need of money
anyway.
This is a country of geniuses. We break records
and standards for the fun of it.
The point that stuck
with me, apart from the pleasant smell of the fresh
apple pie going into the oven,
was that this man
was probably still out there somewhere in Paris
or Woodstock, Brantford or London.
And that on various days
he would go into hardware stores in whatever town he was
passing through, by bus or train, Greyhound or CN,
cheap overcoat, glasses probably, worn leather briefcase,
and he would see his logo sitting on rows
& rows of tins: white, black, blue, red, orange, taupe
& yellow paints.
That's my logo, he would say to himself;
pal, I designed that sucker.

Hugh came over from Rosshire, Scotland, with his parents
in 1843.
They settled outside of Galt. Hugh went off
to San Francisco for the gold rush in 1857.
He kept
a journal of the gold rush sojourn (the trains, camps,
men in sweaty shirts baking bread over open fires)
and wrote a book about Galt
which was serialized in the *Galt Reporter.*

Hugh was a big, slow man,
very precise, intelligent,
but a big man,
very slow to get upset about anything
but firm as a rock.
Tall. Thick white beard in later years
which he washed every morning. A strong man. His father
would carry a sack of freshly milled flour 6 miles from Ayr
back to the Galt farm once a month.
Hugh always wore a dark
suit & a white shirt with a dark tie. He married Christie
Ferguson, the best-looking of the Ferguson girls
and the smartest.
They had 3 children,
all sons, Lorne, Howard, and my mother's father, Duncan.
Duncan took after Hugh but was a lot more flamboyant.

The long dark wood model of the boat Hugh came over
on in 1843, a model that he carved with a jackknife
in his later years
after they moved to Water Street

(the house where my mother was raised
after she left White Plains)
that large dark boat
c/ right down to the rigging, guns painted bronze,
boat painted black,
is now in the study area of my sister's house in Cleveland. Set
on a large shelf – it looks out over the blue waters
of Lake Erie.

San Francisco didn't bring in very much money:
some ingots
that Hugh had made into a gold belt buckle which he later gave
to Christie,
showing if nothing else a flair for occasion.

After he came back from California, he went into the insurance
business. He was a member of the Gore Insurance Company
in Galt,
advanced the company, became its president;
and was the first man in the history of Galt for whom the Gore
flew its flag.
Impressive. But at the back of my mind
there seems to have always been an archetype of Hugh
as a
large, slow man, very intelligent but extremely calm.

I'm very thin and restless myself.
I can hear a butterfly beat its wings at a 100 feet.

But look, I confess, even this recent gold rush in Brazil
they call the 'Big Rat' appeals to me. I'd like to bring home
a few gold buckles myself.

59

My uncle who would never
pay our rent,
after my father fell
from the top of a steeple,
collected stamps
                but later
after the death of my aunt, married
an ex-hooker from Guelph
forgot his pharmacy and went insane.

My mother said:
'He went insane because he sold the store.'

My sister said:
'It must have been the woman; the impact
of being suddenly alone
with someone he didn't really know.'

Our minister disagreed:
'I think he simply reached that point
where he felt his soul lurch in his hands
and come undone
                twelve years
away from his family's church.'

But actually it was because of the stamps;
they had always been a sort of Utopian meadow,
what he would do when he found the time;
and suddenly after all those years
behind the counter, the energy fell out of what
they were supposed to stand for.

My mother found him in the London asylum
wearing a white shirt and trousers,
trying to make an imaginary map
out of remembered octagons and squares
of kings he'd never met
                        and famous ports
he'd always meant to visit,

            to pull them together into something useful
as his first wife,
dead eleven years, would say to him,
'Lorne, can't you fix that cupboard door a bit?'
And of course he would.
                        I told you at the beginning
it was the stamps that drove him crazy;
they were the linchpin
                        of all his other parts.

DUNCAN COMING NORTH THROUGH A 1,000 ISLANDS

1

Duncan was one of those lean young men who went down to Buffalo
to enter Dental College, lived in a small hotel and ate porridge;

after a while the fierce young Scot opened up a solid practice
in White Plains, c/w a German hygienist, married and acquired
a large house.
            I guess he was a good dentist, he was famous
for deft extractions,
but he was a collector and naturally restless:
bits of knowledge, odd expressions,
the invention of a new sewer grating,
the history of railways.

I think he was happy east of the Catskills, with the cold Lakes
of Ontario at a distance behind him,
                              e.g.
Quebec defeated by English Canada & English Canada defeated
by the slowness of investment to develop the West.
                                        But

Duncan did well in White Plains,
white buildings and men with moustaches fixing the roads,
he prospered, married a second time, took a trip to England
and stayed lean & restless.

Buffalo, New York, Detroit & White
Plains were easy,
but growing oranges in Florida stopped Duncan
dead in his tracks with 3 unexpected frosts in a row.

White & green with blue water,
gulf, keys, spits, crawfish, the orange farm, 3 frosts.

Duncan came north again to the farm in Quebec with a red roof
that I saw in the colour photograph
                                        white in winter,
and back to Galt: the Scottish hub set on the Grand River
with its railway bridges, and old granite buildings. He took a night-
watchman's job at Massey-Harris;
                                        it was over before he had
finished, but it wasn't such a bad way to end:
                                        a calendar
of quiet evenings to devote to his remarkable collection
of steel engravings, the odd leather-bound copy of Hooker.

Hooker? I once said to my mother, interested in the word,
is that about fishing?

Duncan began to relax at 72,
slept with a revolver under his pillow, a principle,
memorized
every type of stone commonly found in Maryland on a bet.

I used to sit on Duncan's knee
when I was a child and collect the small metal stick-back foil
wraps from his plugs of pipe tobacco.

He had been married 3 times but would always be in love
with his first wife, my mother's mother.
He had been to Germany and been proposed to by a countess.
He had been stopped by the RCMP who had investigated
his truckload of wooden butterboxes
and found hundreds of books.
Duncan was a romantic rationalist.
The orange farm in Florida was one of his few mistakes.

My father spoke better Latin, and was more athletic
but my father was always away with the Greeks.
                                                    Always
trying to slip off his tweed jacket and sail
into some blue Mediterranean harbour
in the 4th Century B.C. Just to see exactly
how they put up the sails on one of their galleys.

Duncan was tangible and practical and accurate.
Even though I associated him with cities and places
I had never been, like Berlin, White Plains, Montreal,
Florida. I had a bearskin rug from Trois Rivières,
elk horns from somewhere out west.

Duncan migrated a lot. I liked that. We used to go fishing
together in the summer in the afternoons, and he told me
a story about whales.

            I started with matchboxes when I was 4½.
I collect birds, ideas, and relatives.

GALT ARTEFACTS, 1952, SEALED IN A MEMORY DISC

You would probably need a church
where the grandchildren of the bruised but victorious
lift up their heads in exultation,
Knox's, perhaps, & Dalton's drugstore,
                                    a YMCA,
several local butchers, a Main Street bookstore,
& some nighthawks
sailing out after 7 o'clock over the houses
on the west side of the Grand.
                            These entities are more
permanent than Metropolitan newspaper headlines, more
substantial than Napoleon's white horse, or
the Mona Lisa,
            although not permanent forever.

            Artefacts turn up everywhere and have an odd way
of staying in memory,
                    like coding devices or lights at traffic
intersections.
            You can handle artefacts. They have a smell,
and even a taste. Wood, metal,
                            leather, clay. They have odd
little dents, nicks
            & bruises. Sometimes you will notice
a patch of red like a girl's blush
                            on the wooden top of an
old bureau,
            or a pale fingerprint on the dark red laminated
section of a brass telescope.

                    Even the big rusty cannons in the park
which the farm boys lean an elbow on
                                        to have their picture
taken by an obliging sister
                              serve some purpose, although
not as much as buses.
                        A lot of the Portuguese have been
out of work since winter, one of the 3 main factories
has closed down.
                    But there is something timeless about these
towns that survives even the injustice
                                        of a highway change
or the conversion of a sand-washed granite bank
                                          into a ferny
restaurant specializing in brome duck.

                    Meanwhile, telephones work,
gas is 39.4 a litre,
the local opera house has such good acoustics
you can hear a pin drop from the 2nd balcony,
and the only murder victims are raccoons.

                    Plus you can't knock that casual turmoil
of a river where the Baptists
used to hold their children
                              above the white water,
or the way the seagulls hover
                              above the river's surface
when you throw them a piece of bread,

brushing at the brown water
with their pink feet & rising up to catch the light.

FLOOD WALLS

Water Street was where our parents lived across from each other
before they were married.
                    Arnold was born in Mexico,
artist parents, Scottish. Florence was born in New York,
more affluent.

It was where Duncan had lived before moving to White Plains,
after which he bought an orange farm in Florida
had 3 atypical frosts,
                    an astronomical disturbance perhaps,
and came home laughing about the weather.

It was where Mary stayed after she came back from Mexico.

        After my mother's death,
                    Water Street & these stories
became a floating avenue of mustard yellow bricks,

CP Hotels, & elephants & death, of course, & time,

& Lorne's insanity which put him in a white suit.
                                        Not just
social anecdotes or my interest in geography,
but how their stories stand out like rowboats in blue water
with men & women sketching the clouds.

Of a tumult in time, let's say,
of hearts & trains,

of or beside a river, bridges,
                    A Water Street.

Mazatlan is a fishing village,
                              now ½ resort,
½ working people. My father was born there. His father,
                                                    James
Warren Donnell, was a photographer. I think of my father's
progenitor walking along the beach in Mazatlan.
                                        The sun is a
hot yellow in a blue sky. There are some comfortable
houses and some poor slums close to the beach.
                                        James Warren
is poor also. Yesterday he spent hours
working on a photograph of 2 men fishing from a rowboat.
                                                    Other
recent photographs include some portraits of his wife, Mary,
several slow exposures of white sun/salt bleached
driftwood, a visiting bandit with diagonal x cartridge belts,
or at least he claimed to be a bandito, fishing shacks,
weathered grey, usually against a soft light of early dawn.
Some pictures of dark spring storms.
                              This photograph of 2 men
fishing in a rowboat probably won't sell. Glass plate,
colour. Only the occasional studio portrait of a tourist,
loose shirt, poplin jacket, travelling with his wife,
seems to sell and bring in a few dollars for cornmeal,
cornbread, fish (which he could catch if he wanted to)
and basic sandy vegetables. Most of these people have never
seen American money. Pesos, notes, bright funny pastel
colours.

My father's mother, Mary Cavers, is sitting on a torn
deck chair outside the fishing hut they rent for 5 dollars

a month. They could almost afford to buy it. A kitchen
with a sink but no running water. They use a hose to fill
the sink and put boards across it & close up the windows
with blankets to make a darkroom. He does several glass
plates at a time. They are in their 30s.

          Even the money
for James Warren's tobacco cuts into their modest budget.
The glass plates and the money for her oil paints cost more.
Burnt umber – 65¢, chrome blue – 65¢, Venetian red – 75¢.
A different manufacturer.

        This woman carried my father
for nine months in her belly in the warm Mexican sunshine.

                    She
was Scottish also, but from Ayr, near Galt. A farm,
but she was well-read. Not an original artist so much

             as a
brilliant copyist. Often abandoned the small tubes of paint
for her own formula of egg yolk and pigment.
Grinding the dark blue herself
for a specific copy
from Peter Paul Rubens.

       James W. liked photographing
by day, late afternoon perhaps. Mary liked painting
by lamplight.

    It increased concentration,

           allowed lush
detail to become perfect. My father had that tendency
in his own character.

      Not too many quotes from his father,
but something of his mother's method, her meticulous sense of
form,

    exact view or shade of meaning. James Warren was a
tall good-looking man with reddish hair and a thick moustache.
He was often out at the cantinas in the evening,

           although

whether he actually chased other women or not is debatable.
Mary left him, just like a plucky middle-class farm girl
from Ayr.

Came north with my father through San Francisco
where she'd been married, and up through New York. And
then back to Galt. Homestead is heartland.
Mary was a very beautiful woman.
She died in Toronto in her late 50s, 2 weeks before my father
graduated from college.

This story is really about how I met John Paul Getty on the street in San Francisco one day; but it begins, in a way, with my ruminations on the nature of family, because that's what I'd been thinking about, not millionaires or stock-exchanges; I'd been calling up various passages from texts and magazine articles like a slightly fried computer-assisted free-lance writer, putting a fact-spread together, for several weeks, before the sunny afternoon when I saw Getty on the street, and just flash, walked up and spoke to him. I'm mentioning this because I want you to understand that I'm a serious person, I'm not the kind of guy who just walks up to people on the street and talks to them for a joke. I'm a spontaneous person but there's usually a reason behind my spontaneity.

It was a Wednesday afternoon and I'd been at Alvin's Clam & Oyster House for lunch. Just a cheap lunch, San Francisco clam chowder, crusty white Portuguese bread and the daily special which was ocean bass served with a little pile of marinated vegetables. I was walking east on Kaminsky Street, sauntering along by myself somewhat moodily, kicking at the odd debris, a crumpled napkin, a pop bottle top, with my hands in my pockets, feeling very relaxed and somewhat moody at the same time.

There was a large black Lincoln Continental, tinted windows and two chrome exhaust pipes, pulled up in front of Dubuth's Cigar Store across the street from the Sunshine Grill. I paused to look at the car before I was up to it, and as I paused a very strong-faced elderly man, soft white hair, dark suit, slightly bent, came walking out of the store, with a cane under his arm and a box of cigars in his hand. The box wasn't wrapped and it was a soft golden-brown shade of box with a gold seal, some sort of flower, I think, with bits of red for petals, on top of the lid. I recognized him at once because the woman I live with, Esmeralda, had just been reading an article in *Fortune* about his collection of French Impressionists.

Something seized me, I don't know what it was. The 2 Strohs I'd had with my lunch, Jimmy Mainwaring's conversation about losing some money in Santa Anita last week, maybe just a sudden childish desire to ride in Getty's car, but I walked straight over to him as the chauffeur, a sardonic-looking black man in his 40s, was holding open the large dark blue- & beige-lined rear door for him.

'John Paul Getty,' I said, throwing open my arms, not too wildly, and smiling broadly and cheerfully like a Harvard graduate greeting someone he had shared a lab with in 4th year a long time ago.

Getty batted about ⅕ of one eye, paused imperceptibly and looked at his chauffeur, who immediately straightened up and looked enquiringly, no, menacingly at me, and the financier shifted the box of cigars to put it under his far arm.

'Mr. Getty,' I said very politely, now standing about 2 feet from his left elbow, 'I'm Arnold Donnell's son, I'm a botanist now.' He paused for a second and the chauffeur started to speak. The chauffeur stepped forward between us or almost between us.

If only the CIA had protected Kennedy this thoroughly, I thought to myself; that was my first mental reaction apart from being slightly intimidated by the chauffeur. I'm a typical white Anglo-Saxon intellectual, and Black men over 6' intimidate me even at parties. My other mental reaction was the scene in *Annie Hall* where Allen is pacing up and down the room brooding and fussing over the Kennedy assassination, and Carol Kane, in a shapeless grey sweater, is sitting, legs folded like a San Francisco flower beneath her, at the foot of the bed. I can't remember if the bed is made or not, but it's not important.

The chauffeur spoke shortly and bluntly into this daze like a small Tom Waits' klaxon. He said, 'Get your ass out of here, Sonny.' The guy didn't even call me bud, or bimbo or asshole, which in New York is an almost affectionate term. He called me Sonny. As if I were about 4 years old and my worn tweed jacket and slightly stained tan chinos were a security blanket. Getty seemed to be about to get in the car. The back seat was voluminous. I thought he must feel lost back there by himself. I could see an outlet for an electric razor, a hook for a pants or suit press, and a closed panel door which I presumed concealed a handy/andy bar.

The great man paused, half bent over on his way into the voluminous back seat, and straightened up.

'Donnell,' he said, he grunted, his mouth was soft and gentle but very precise, worn and folded, as if it had considered millions of hundred-dollar bills and names of French paintings and commands to servants for more years than I had even been alive. 'Arnold Donnell,' he said, 'you've got a book out.' He stood facing me. The chauffeur stepped aside and looked at the sidewalk. There was nothing moving on the sidewalk, but he looked at it as if there were. A snail, maybe, or a small displaced wood slug or an urban beetle.

'Yes,' I said, 'it's a botanist's notebook really, it's about Central Park in New York, it's not the kind of book I usually write. I'm David. Arnold was my father.'

He shifted his weight to one foot and grunted. 'I know,' he said a little brusquely, as if I had been chiding him for his memory. 'I knew your father in college.'

'It's not a textbook,' I said hurriedly, 'it's more of a botany watcher's book.'

'I know the book,' he snapped. He was becoming irritable with me. I talk too much.

'My wife's secretary bought a copy of it. I saw the book,' he intoned, 'in an advertisement. She bought it. We have it around the house or maybe,' he paused, a man who likes to be exact in all things, a trait I like to flatter myself I also have, 'it's out at the summer farm.'

'Yes,' I said. I wanted to mention the title of the book, which is *The Trees & Bushes of Central Park,* but decided that I shouldn't. I'd be forcing it. He actually had a copy of the book, at home, wherever that was, or at the summer place.

It was a very beautiful day and I was amazed. I didn't really trust him. I thought he was being polite.

'It's not very good,' I said.

'I haven't read it,' he shrugged. He remarked this as if it were an observation on the weather.

'But if you don't think it's very good,' he went on, probably hungering for one of the cigars, 'why did you write the god-damn thing? Besides,' he continued more gently, 'you should never write a book and publish it and then say it isn't very good. If you don't stand behind what you do, you'll confuse people and they won't like you. And you won't,' he turned to the chauffeur, 'George...,' he said.

'... learn anything about yourself,' George, who was standing quietly at attention, said with a sudden unexpected smile.

'Exactly,' said the great man, 'you won't learn anything about yourself. You'll become willy-nilly and shiftless as a scared dog.'

The chauffeur smiled with satisfaction almost as if he were smiling on behalf of Getty, not doing it for him but smiling almost as a form of unconscious role play.

'Your father was crazy.' I almost thought it was the chauffeur speaking for a second, but it was Getty, the voice hoarse and unmistakably Boston-Mid-Atlantic-California. I was becoming flustered. I wondered idly if my shirt-tail was hanging out.

'Your father was crazy about the Greeks,' he said, looking at me kindly now. He appeared to have fond memories of my father. I thought this was good, that he might give me a ride in his car after all.

My new name is Wilson. Angus Wilson. I was born in Canada. I'm Scottish and I was born in Canada, but I live in San Francisco now because it's easier to get around. I'm 34. I'm slightly overweight, but I'm not gay. I have opportunities to score in this town like you wouldn't believe, but I don't do very much with them. I like cars and old buildings. I go to movies and I drift around quite a bit.

'He was a specialist in Homer,' I said, 'he didn't know anything about flowers. My mother knew a lot about flowers, she was crazy about them, she was a great gardener.'

'Homer,' the great man mused. The sun was falling on us and it was very warm. I thought he must be extremely warm in his dark wool suit, but if he was he didn't show it. The chauffeur was also quite fully dressed.

Apparently Homer still commanded a certain amount of clout, tradition, the span of history. I have an occasional fondness for things that have been proven to be of real worth, real quality, Renoir's fatuous paintings of women bathing, no sex, not nearly as good as his paintings of women at the opera, dressed, formal, bourgeois animals seeking the pleasure of social attention and social stature, basking in the warm dark approval of the enraptured theatre. Homer was still important, still something on which to base an argument, or interrupt a discussion over afternoon cocktails.

I didn't mention Arnold A. Donnell's bizarre fascination with Heath-Stubbs' private life, or his theories about the novels of Emily Brontë.

'He lectured on Homer, down here at Berkeley, before the students painted the university black and moved to the beach,' I said.

'Yes, well I don't think I heard him,' he said kindly. His mouth was actually quite fresh, his eyes were a little rheumy, cataracts perhaps, but his mouth was quite fresh and his voice was strong. He was a little bit like a llama in an expensive dark wool suit.

'We were in the same residence,' he said, 'people called them residences. I talked to your father a number of times about going into business. That's what Homer would have done, even if it's true that he was as blind as a bat.

'But your father was adamant. He started off with Greek history, all that stuff about boats and the Mediterranean. They're still into that,' he asided to the chauffeur who was paying some discreet attention to the details of the conversation, 'and then your father wound up with Homer. Quite a vocation,' he said, straightening up a little straighter and signalling George.

The royal cigar box was becoming heavy. Each long perfect green-shaded panetella like the perfect turd of a royal sausage maker.

'I'm driving east,' he said, as if he was commandeering the large dark Lincoln himself. 'Can I give you a lift?'

Let me be honest and tell you I was deeply tempted. I thought it would be quite wonderful to ride along for a few blocks in all that dark sumptuous luxuriance. Reality entered in the form of the Fish & Chip shop sign next to the Sunshine Grill. 'No,' I said, 'I'm just meeting someone for a drink and some conversation about birds.'

'Oh,' he said with interest, 'you do birds too, eh? That's good, that's very good.

'There's a lot we don't know about birds,' he said to George, and he got into the plush back of the limousine and put the box of cigars beside him on the seat. George smiled at me perfunctorily and walked around to the driver's side.

Getty put down the back window. 'Your father's still alive, isn't he?' he said. 'Somewhere in New England?' He was gentle but he looked as if he was closing a business deal on a painting.

I didn't have the heart, maybe inclination is a better word, to tell him the whole thing had been a jest.

'No,' I said, truthfully, 'he's dead, he died 5 or 6 years ago.'

'I'm sorry to hear it,' he said. 'Say hello to your mother for me. I never met her.'

'No,' I said, 'she died several years ago. In Chicago.'

'Well,' he said, wearily, 'keep up with the botany. It's good stuff. And the birds too.'

The big limo drove off almost as suddenly as the back window went up and there I was, standing in the middle of Kaminsky Street with the sun pouring down and this Hispanic guy I know to talk to coming out of the Sunshine Grill folding up a newspaper and looking around for a cab. There aren't very many cabs on Kaminsky Street but I didn't call across to him. I stood looking in the window of the cigar store for a little while. Then I went in and spent $4.50 on a Romeo y Julieta because I thought my little prank was an occasion to celebrate.

It was quite beautiful, really. He'd stopped and talked to me and been friendly simply on the basis of having known my father; better, having gone to college with him. My father knew a lot of people at college, but that's beside the point. Getty was an astute man, not just a rich scion. He was a shrewd tested old trader among traders. A leisurely yacht among rowboats. And he'd stopped and been friendly simply on the basis of family. It made me feel very young for some reason. It made me feel about 4 years old.

I lit up the Romeo y Julieta and walked up Kaminsky to Hennepin, and up Hennepin to the top of the hill where I could watch the lobster boats coming in. It was still sunny and I didn't feel the sadness I'd been feeling for several weeks. There's more salt in the air in San Francisco than there is in my beloved Chicago. I felt reflective but I didn't feel stuck anymore. San Francisco's like that: the weather gets fairly cool at times, but it always has a certain lift. There's a spontaneity in the air, and spontaneity is amazing because it makes us forget about certain aspects of the past. I smoked the Romeo y Julieta without inhaling it, meaning I just puffed and scratched my head and thought about New England while I watched the lobster boats coming in. I'm 34 now and as I told you before I like cars and old buildings a lot. I also like big names and dark wool suits, but I guess I don't like them as much as I thought.

77

1

Katharine used to put raw steaks
in front of me and sing Puccini. Harris
compared the heart of the Prime Minister to a drowsy weasel.
A young girl appeared in the daily newspapers around this time
giving private violin recitals in the nude at a salon:
photographers came and knelt at her feet with cynical smiles.
We experience several problems when we come to the city
with our torn blue work-shirts and yellow straw in our hair.
Roland Barthes' *Mythologies* makes a number of things plain
about the importance of the human smile.
K said she and a friend were going to a Mendelssohn concert
at Massey Hall,
                    so Carol and I drove up to the farmhouse
to see Tom and Linda.
Harold was there. The weather was lovely. So was Cynthia.
Martin and Wendy have a child who plays with ducks.
Alison used to sing *'Down with the bourgeoisie'* at the crest
of orgasm when she lived with Tom in New York;
but no one knows if Martin's gay or not. Casual. Removed.
Maybe Martin likes photographing men because they're attractive.

What can you do in a country like Canada
besides plant wheat and develop copper mines?
Tom browned a magnificent leek pie to go with the back ribs
and farmer's bread Carol and I brought up from the city.
Cynthia made a great soup with tomatoes and dill.
After supper we sat out on the large back farmhouse deck.
Harold and Martin took turns comparing the moon
to something fabulous
but the moon looked down yellow and cool & said nothing.

Back inside, Linda played albums of Schönberg and Dvořák.
We told stories over Harold's whisky and smoked
2 joints the size of broomsticks.
Then everyone got dressed up as someone famous. Hemingway.
Einstein. Napoleon. History bleeds into our best photographs
but no one wanted to be Egerton Ryerson. I was Kerouac
although I don't have that beautiful sad look around the eyes.
Carol made a toga out of a red velvet curtain.
She was discernibly naked and beautiful underneath
except for a pair of Tom's boxer shorts.

'O well, darling,' Cynthia said to Martin,
'it's all opera, isn't it?'
But she took off her sweater, lifting it up over her blonde head
with her long stomach pulled in
and said that she was Marilyn Bell and about to swim the lake.

Suddenly there K was in the middle of the living room up from her shower with dramatic blue eyes and a stiff white tuxedo dress-shirt open to her waist.
The Argentinian tango is all about emotional attitudes.
I try daily to develop more socially conscious reflexes.
But K got to my silly wombat and made me feel slightly guilty.
Dante's shadow is as lustrous as a ripe cheese.
I come from a Scottish family in Galt.
The Amish still pass through my head with their terrifying black hats like Sunday on wagons.
Social groups tend to collect each other's cigar labels.
The photographers knelt at Beatrice's feet with cynical smiles.
Not us.
My mouth is as innocent as yellow corn.

'Tell K I'm 95% innocent,' I said to Harris, 'after you put your pants back on. And stop waving that American flag out the window.'

The Count di Agriona had mines of alum,
just like salt or copper mines, and his inflated pricing in 1594
made up for the lack of interest on his loan to the State of Venice.
Interesting.
I have a friend who used to work for *Time* as a photographer.
Joyce memorized a long passage from Edgar Quinet
and used it in the *Wake:*
Fraîches et riantes comme aux jours des batailles.
K loves pasta with Gorgonzola and ham but this is academic.
The peaches of St. Marys will be ripe by August.
Nostalgia is olfactory and visual as well as tactile.
Eggplant requires garlic and olive oil and black pepper.
The leek pie was good cold the next morning for breakfast.
These are beautiful people with too much pungent tobacco.
Carol was sitting with her toga draped around her shoulders

talking to Harris about New Orleans in the 1920s.
I would like to write something as simple as *The Nephew.*
Martin got another cold beer & some sausage
and went out to the barn
to observe the Guernsey giving birth to a blue-eyed calf.
I am 26 now; more or less.
My eyes are as sharp as F.16/500. I am calm,
and my mouth is still as innocent as a fresh pear.

II

DRIVING

DRIVING

Little Pawling

You pass between two long rock shields, granite that's been
                              rained burnt orange,
as you approach the highway overpass to my mother's birth-
place in White Plains, NY.
                         The exit for Little
Pawling & the Saw Mill Parkway are on your left. We take 684
& head toward Brewster. You drive. I am asleep.

I wanted to see White Plains & walk down its quiet Main Street
& look at the house where my mother was born & raised;

but it's late afternoon, & we agree to do this next time.

White Plains is a family name for pork roasts & Sunday beans,

but I even like Katonah, a blue sunset, a posh grocery
store across from an Amtrak station,
                              weathered red platforms,
cement & skinheads
with tattooed ear lobes. 'Make mine a cross.' Lamb

chops, potatoes, eggs, butter, milk, American chocolate chip
cookies, yogurt, a dozen Pabst Blue Ribbon, fresh green
beans, & farmer's bread.
                    You know me pretty well by now.
I don't gain weight very much, but I eat a lot.
Like a horse.

Larchmont

         This slow-motion passing of White Plains
& Little Pawling has turned me around. Changed my socks,
rolled up my sleeves.

My St. Marys childhood drifts up beside me in a black DeSoto.
Formal dining-room habits.
                    A Fats Waller album
I haven't thought of for years. An old newspaper headline.
Some tools lying out on the back porch. Photographs.
                                  But
the image of my mother at 15 or so – that I form driving down
a slope to the fish market –
                  while moody
& oblique
           is almost as clear as yesterday's photograph of a
white-suited Woodrow Wilson speaking at an Algonquin supper,

or that photograph Ellen says she likes of Duncan
                        young
& rawboned & handsome, in a cane chair on the back sunporch
at White Plains.
            That one says, '1919. The summer
after the war.'

You can get fresh crab on a kaiser in Larchmont
& eat it beside the Atlantic.

(Chocolate-brown Audi. German engine. 1985
Italian carburetor.)
The sun pulsing down
through the open sun-roof, my summer laziness,
2 kids on the street skateboarding in long pink shorts;

your hair, thick, sweet;
her breasts under the soft cotton sundress
low over one shoulder, that damp spot below
the clavicle where I kissed. Disturbs me.
I get my hair
cut short at a barbershop on Monroe Street & a clean shave
as smooth as a baby's bum.
Come back to the car shirt off
in the hot sun, khaki shorts bulging with green peas
in the summer mote dust
& one rough thread
rubbing against my sunburned thigh.

(How can you write about skin & involve family photographs
& rage or despair in the same sentence? This is asking
the horse to run in slow motion so the photographer
with a blond moustache can click a shutter.)

Don't think about it so much.
Just/do it.

Louis Armstrong said he liked Beiderbecke's playing
the best: because Bix had the most ingredients.

I loved you the most. You were ineffable
but you had glory dancing at your fingertips.

I can hear the hip-sway,
                              pink slip
& rustle of a late Billie Holiday song on the West German
car radio, driving through Goshen,

although Lady Day didn't start recording until the Dirty '30s.
When hotels got rough & Memphis grocery stores sold ham
sandwiches for 5¢ each.
                              This gestalts it for me
probably more than any archive would. I can see my mother

& Duncan standing out on the L-shaped front porch
in White Plains,
                    after supper perhaps,
                                        discussing boys,
perfume, dances & Galt.

Duncan is talking vaguely about parties on Lake Boats
if she moves back to Galt
(but she mustn't wear lipstick.
O shit.)

Maybe the soft voice in the song isn't black,
maybe it was white, my mother's turned around,
                                        an upstate New
York voice with the German vowels still evident
                                        that lasted
until Roosevelt's final speeches. Or King's, perhaps.

But it drew *me* into its moody blues like buttered grace. A
touch & feel to it.
                    Pale gravel against the right fender.

Darien

        Darius or Darien. There's a pizzeria
with a good bar next door.
              That slow Billie Holiday song
put me in a frame. I'm hungry & want to eat. But there are
             several other forgotten tunes,

an old parade piece
or private military schoolboy's marching song,
with one young boy, cowlick brushed back, water-slick,
blue eyes eager as a long-nosed beagle scenting partridge,
licking his mouth desperately to get some spit ready
for a first *ta-ta-tataa ta-ta-tataa* of the required bugle.

Photographs.
tafts cants cavers fergusons woodwards gaudières.
                  Of you
at a Boston prom age 16½. Low-cut satin. Flowers.
Glasses of punch. Smiling like a leggy young Merle Oberon

with no view of the future with a face: my stepfather,
hopping lurching demented drunk chicken, sodden rooster,
around the Galt kitchen with a towel over his bleeding
hand, breaking windows.

That clear soft brass sound lifts the rawboned young man out
of his cane porch chair & sends him back to the lake
                     to his
second wife. Or was it his third?

Why would some rural schoolteacher call this piece of fly shit
Darien?
        Answer:
Because it's on a ridge, stupid.

Driving home now after Lake Waccabuc,
                                        that
tough plaintive strain Billie articulates so well,
stamping her feet,
throwing her gardenias to the audience,
                                    of always needing
A Man,

has been replaced by a kind of jazz.
                            Burnished brass alto
saxophones, snaky snare drums, solar keyboard, smoky, dark
& moody.

            This smoke is what pulls me into the city & raunchy
places   my mother probably never went even briefly,
with her first lipstick & some Player's cigarettes to visit
a cheeky friend at a girl's residence.

Broadway & 10th, the River Café, Ketchum's,
the 14th Ward where Miller lived, Main Street,
& of course the Docks,
                        where the Lebanese once had
a whole culture of their own   before they moved to
Brooklyn.

Gananoque

Turned around & coming back now, saxophones,
the Motherwell show,
I think about the fields & barns & silos
& houses we pass. Rural greens & yellows.
Not very much difference perhaps unless you drive south as far
as Kentucky.
But this musing
about evening porches & swing era dance music
gets interrupted at Gananoque, high above the 1,000 Islands
where we have our summer luggage methodically searched
& a discussion ensues about 2 cartons of Camels,
filter, lights, & a copy of James Salter's magnificent *A Sport
and a Pastime.*

The border of a page is usually white.

I can imagine the afternoon foxes outside of Syracuse or Albany
sniffing at dark brush;
soft nighthawks
swooping down over the St. Marys quarry. Pale stone. Salt
mine. Dark cherry
pit. Dinner in Kingston. Cool sleep.
(You hated pigeons. I love them. It is dark now. ½ moon.)

Odessa

              Tail-lights disappearing around the dark curve
up ahead.
            Roadside underbrush a soft dark blue. ½ moon.
Warm hazy summer. Invisible flowers.

Tafts, Ohio.
         I had almost forgotten
my mother was a beautiful niece who collected letters,
photographs, cuff-links, clear myths of the illustrious:
starched & well-brushed grand-uncles
who smoked Cuban cigars & ran for the Presidency.

I wanted a time frame that would make my mother's image
more intense. More specific.
               So I have circled her birth-
place like a soft-mouthed red-haired cocker spaniel flushing
grouse.

Tail-lights pinpoint bouncing on the dark curve & split.
Over-nite trailer to the left & a Penn train. That light
                        at evening
                          crossings.
Ore cars. Painted letters & #s.
                Railway men are never
fond of Mozart. Maybe jigs & reels. Night

raccoon playing with a tin can lid by the side of the road.
Almost invisible.

Don Valley

We come down through St. Clair Avenue
where some of the Gelatis & striped-awning Cappuccino cafés
are open late.
      I could never
share this with you. What I did share was St. Marys & Galt,
      uncles & grandfathers,
      solariums & cornfields,

but we both moved to Toronto years ago.
      Bathurst & Davenport.
The main avenues dark & wet impressionist parade grounds.
      No
Billie Holiday songs on the radio. A piano concerto
by some obscure German.
      Wet splashes on the asphalt
reflecting pale yellow streetlights.
Cézanne would have loved this city on a rainy night.

I keep some of the childhood memories & discard others.
      Notes,
letters, photographs.
Like the raccoon playing with a tin can lid
in the dark.
      I was so hurt by your death
that I had a savage grudge against this city. Foolish
of me.
      Why not have a grudge against Little Pawling?
St. Clair afternoons, or Parkdale,
where you lived for the last 10 years
of your life?
      The great white elephant buildings of the CNE?
The Roncesvalles car line. How the blue conductors

used to shout out – '. . . Fer manAUGH.'

                                Or Granowska's where
the solid Polish women make the best mixed flan in Canada?
Or the place in Goshen
                    where the man taking care of the bar
said, 'Time, well now, time is funky.' And scrubbed the zinc
with a mordant expression.
                       And I said, No, time is driving.
On a good day when there's not too much traffic.
Driving around in a circle until you come back to where you
started, unbent,
& praise even the highway overpass,
                           the raccoon playing
in the dark, or the sparrows on the morning telephone wire.

III

UP FROM THE RIVER

Sofas

      St. Marys, stone town, has a lot to offer.
                                  Calm.
Raccoons & cool in the summer. That
burnished colour of the sun on green-veined yellow leaves
where texture mindlessly cups drunk light;

my favourite bridge, the creek, a cleft giant willow fishing
place with rocks. This is idyllic.
But no mothers kitchens the German *kitsch kinde kinder*,

and no fathers living rooms Greek texts sawdust shavings
or Victorian paperweights.

No mothers, no fathers. Maybe a cousin or two.

There are broken living-room sofas that remind you of aunts.

There are fields and the moon, familiar places,
a great restaurant,
& some sunlit nearby farms.

Pheasants

We lived on Wellington Hill up from the river,
and the Scottish settlements spread as far north as Goderich.

My father taught Classics at the local Collegiate
and didn't go snowshoeing anymore.
                                    My life was extremely
free. I wasn't allowed to run wild, but I could come & go
as I liked.
                A well-settled stone town. But there were wild
pheasants in the backyard in winter,
cornfields, barns, quarries, & ½-ton
pickup trucks filled with lumber.
                                    I came and went as I liked,
imagining those pheasants in the breakfast room
stamping the snow off their pronged feet;

lazy in summer,
I collected milkweed pods
with my sister up by the sleepy railway tracks.

Opera

      We had a beautiful opera house. (Still
there. As a matter of fact, they've been raising money

to have it restored.) Art committee events, plays
from Toronto. My father listened to the opera every Saturday

afternoon with a console radio in our big living room. A
plaza of sound in a small town where raccoons would wander

at night along Trout Creek. For my part, I would listen
to these huge-lunged Italian tenors sock it to fey Puccini

like a string of oranges exploding in a brass French horn,
and imagine the rich Italian words as a mating dance,

like birds, or the 'billing and cooing' of parents
before they disappear on a Friday evening,

flirtation as a preface before enormous late-night suppers,
pasta tonatto, Bolognese, Milanese, Alfredo, pizzaiola,

like the different chapters in Mrs. Genovese's cookbook.

Then I would imagine these sopranos & tenors wandering
home to sleep like bedsprings playing Ravel's *Bolero*.

DiMaggio

Let me confess. I've always liked Einstein,
but I've never been very good
                                    at algebra or gym. I smoked dope
in washrooms & thought about crows & Joe DiMaggio in class.

While various teachers conjugated Latin verbs or talked about
chemical compounds.
                        I masturbated late at night
dreaming about K walking to school in her red plaid skirt,
& bit my pillows like Nabisco shredded wheat with raisins,
brown sugar & milk.

Lipstick

      Obviously it was the colour red, as in blood,
or tail-lights, or lipstick, or the colours of a typical farm,

that acted as a prod or semiotic pin this afternoon.
                                       Playing
with my head,
making me think about St. Marys. Instead of about Toronto
or Galt,
or the various problems in front of me.
                                    Tail-lights
probably, flashing on and off in the dark, up and down
the 9,870 streets and boulevards of Toronto.
                                  Making me
just a little restless, 2 shades reactive.
                                 Thinking,
no doubt, of some argument, some trifle sharp enough
to give this admired head a hangover like blue
& sulphur-
yellow fog. And then the overwhelming nostalgia flips up
like a Jungian photograph.

      That family love is still rich enough
to spread on a piece of bread like butter.

Proust

    Proust was a genius with telescopes.
I have some talent in this direction. Radar sets,
& differently coloured memory spools.
I can roll them up, pale blue, dark wine, laminated,

& unroll them:
      fine oil-rubbed screws, Dutch Hague glass cut
from the sun's prism, smoky tarnished tuba French horn brass;

on various occasions, parking lots, valleys or hills,

from Chekhov's daughters who always have observations about
the weather,
    to how Romeo
gives both harsh families a ripe fig between his fingers
in *Romeo & Juliet.*

    But these telescopes don't always
cope with my basic problem of place. Those trees,
          those
roads. There are days when I can feel my shoulders expand
with exasperation,
      my arms stretch out like trees. When
the desire almost lifts me up out of my present situation

and moves me back into those familiar areas.
A walk along Trout Creek,
which I can see perfectly well in the telescope,
        but
not smell, not feel the wetness of it, through the shade
under the big knotted willow trees, and out past the river,
until suddenly I'm lost in fields of yellow hay. Lost, as
they say, calm, and totally found.

IV

LIGHT PHOTOGRAPHS

There is an old children's song that goes:
'The 24th of May is the Queen's birthday,
Let's all go and play before the close of the day.'
I always thought the Queen in the song was the old Queen, Victoria, whom I had read about and seen at my grandfather's apartment on Blair Road in one of his huge black & white engravings that he collected from innumerable auction sales: surrounded by a black South African regiment and two huge lions. The 24th of May meant fireworks. Roman Candles, Sparklers, Catherine Wheels. The 4th of July, celebrated a short distance south in Michigan and New York, also meant fireworks. I was unaware of the fact that Guy Fawkes Day in England preceded both the 24th and the 4th. I liked the day, occurring at the end of spring and the beginning of summer, simply as an ineffable day, a celebration, a family fireworks night, we always had our own fireworks and I thought of them as coming from China. I had seen photographs in a children's book of fireworks in the shapes of dragons and kites.

My father hadn't been especially fond of fireworks. My father was fond of Herodotus. He was fond of Anaximander, the early Greek scientist who invented the giant mirror which according to myth burned an enemy fleet in the harbour. He was fond of J.W. Turner, some of whose brilliant paintings show ships at anchor with the sun falling, spilling on their stretched sails in so many shades that it looks to a child's eye – and the eye of the London art public at that time – as if the sails were on fire. Ablaze in the harbour.

My father's idea of the 24th of May – and presumably he

had known exactly whose birthday it was (her picture was all over our money, and when we drove over to Buffalo to visit our cousins, there was no way that the Buckwheat Pancake House would accept that money) – was to go for a drive in the country, or Niagara Falls, or even Toronto. I enjoyed this also.

But night and day are as different as cats and potatoes.

The 24th of May as a date on the calendar meant that we were definitely nearing the end of our school year; and, if I didn't have to write my exams, I would be out soon, fishing out of a rowboat on the Grand River, or skivving along the Cedar Creek Road in search of rabbits.

The 24th of May as a night meant that the huge dark blue cobalt sky over Galt, which saw nighthawks in the summer, and star constellations more clearly than they could be seen in Hamilton because Galt had almost no pollution at all at that time, would be lit up from over a hundred or more backyards – we were on a slight hill – with these blue, red, and yellow displays of light. They were called fireworks. But there was never a fire. It was a display of light that we made ourselves, like a Milky Way.

We had cannons in Galt but they were never fired for a public event. The huge weathered stone Armoury across from the bus depot, where my sister occasionally went to dances, usually had a noon-hour drill inspection.

My errant stepfather didn't know much about Turner, but he liked fireworks well enough, and – until we moved, sold the big house and moved to Toronto (hogtown of the midwest, between French Quebec, where the women wore scarves on the street, and the Rockies, where they had real mountain goats) – he would go out and buy, not just in Galt but while he was out driving around on the truck, 15 or 20 dollars' worth of these Roman candles, sparklers, and Catherine wheels. These were fancier than the small-time explosives I bought. And sometimes he would buy rockets, but they couldn't be set off in our big side yard. They had to be taken down to the Grand River and set off like waltzing starbursts over the dark water. With my allowance, or sometimes with an additional 4 dollars that he would give me out of the cracked brown leather wallet he carried, I would go to Buck's Service Station up toward the county line and buy ladyfingers, also the name of a flat spongy cake; 'plain reds,' your average size, just right to roll under a door; and cannon crackers, which were the big guys, almost the size of a shotgun shell.

This would give us a full complement of fireworks for the peaceful evening ahead.

But first I would have the day itself. It was like the beginning of summer. The trees were already green, the flowers were pushing up, the frogs were already croaking like a chorus of aging uncles out at the frog pond on the Cedar Creek Road. Usually there would be a rifle salute downtown at the Armoury, and a well-attended baseball game at Victoria Park down by the river.

Then there would be the evening.

Of course these were *little* bombs, but Victoria wasn't really any more opposed to bombs than George Washington.

The 4th of July comes a little closer to costume duplication, but the fireworks were pretty much the same in both countries. Canadians like eagles, lemonade, and gin, but they don't usually get dressed up in military costumes. My grandfather Duncan would get out his flag on the 4th of July, 48 stars and 13 stripes, this was a flag from White Plains and dated from before Alaska became a State. He would hang this flag quite resplendently out his bay living-room window on Blair Road on a long flag-pole with a large gilt eagle at the top. There were no throngs of people marching past his window, but it was a gesture, and I guess it celebrated the spirit of '76. '76 was the spirit my mother talked to me about when I was a child. But nothing remains in my memory from the picture-books she showed me except Paul Revere, and Washington crossing the Potomac.

We had marching bands in Galt for the 24th of May, but not public, historic marches with people joining in and children running to catch up. These bands celebrated a different kind of spirit than New Orleans. They were Scottish Kiltie Bands, bright with tartan, and equipped with large oompah drums, and loud, sweet pipes that could separate the hawks and the pigeons in mid flight. Most English or Italian descent Canadians hate the sound of the pipes. I love that sound. The bands were good. And they made me very proud to be Scottish. Southwestern Ontario was Scottish and so was I. It was as simple as that. Victoria was a good Queen, Long Live The Queen, and she was certainly long dead. We had our own country, and there was endless land and buckets of peach ice-cream to prove it. I think *this* is what the parades celebrated.

There were evening tattoos with fireworks in the shapes of flags, magical Roman candles, and exploding rockets over the Grand River. Until City Council put a restrainer on the rockets after a hotel close to the river caught fire one year.

These were just little bombs. And the Catherine wheels weren't bombs at all. They were light.

My mother would make lemonade and we would take the fireworks into the garden after supper. My stepfather would put the 3 or 4 rockets aside to take down to the river. I would be put in charge of the Roman candles. RCs, my stepfather would call them. My stepfather called me Buck and Buckaroo. 'Set off the RCs, Buck,' he would say, and I would set them off from 4 or 5 different points in the yard and let them arch, red ball, yellow ball, up in the dark air, and out over the rolling terraces that sloped down to a gravel path above John Street. Everybody would have sparklers. Sometimes my sister's friend Pat. My friend Peter.

My stepfather would walk around and admire the whole event. He thought it was amazing. My sister would tack the Catherine wheels onto the big maple tree at the side of the front porch, or to the sides of the garage across from the vegetable garden.

These were just little bombs. It was like a picnic at night. It was our way of warming up for the tattoo down at Victoria Park. Then my mother would take in the lemonade and the glasses. Nancy would walk her friend Pat home, perhaps. My stepfather and I, and sometimes Peter and Bobby, would take the 3 or 4 rockets we'd put aside earlier, down to the Grand River and set them off, red, blue, and yellow over the dark water. Down there by the river, always optimistic, I would wonder if the professors and dancing girls I liked to imagine, could see our fireworks all the way from Toronto where my father had gone to college.

Willow Creek flows south into Fergus, home of the legendary Shann Dam; the Grand River flows south *from* Fergus, through Elora, where the copper shines after a rain in the Elora Gorge, West Montrose, and Conestogo, willowy as a snake. Then it jogs east, twisting, through the Kitchener and Waterloo area, and comes into Galt, now called Cambridge, wide enough to flood the cellars of the Water Street and Grand Street stores in the spring, but otherwise manageable, calm, no white-edged crests beating against the feet of bridges, but good for fishing, the occasional rowboat or raft, skating in winters, very few drownings take place in Galt. MacPhairn would be one, old Ross MacPhairn's nephew, but he wasn't an adventurous boy, he was a middle-aged drunk.

Then after Galt, now called Cambridge, the Grand River, grand eponym of the Grand Theatre, the Grand Hotel, Wiley & Sons Grand River Camping Supplies, where you get really good long underwear, down vests, bamboo creels, rods, tackle, Primus stoves and hand-warmers, the Grand jogs continually further east, first twisting over to Paris, then down through Brantford, at which point it really makes up its mind, it doesn't want to go west, so it loops over to Onondaga, down through Caladonia, and finally spills itself into Lake Erie south of Dunnville at Port Maitland.

This was at one time a major commercial route. The Grand Trunk Railway system didn't follow the course of the river, although the rails still do at certain points, the Grand Trunk didn't empty into Port Maitland, for example. But there were shipping routes along the Grand, specific hotels where Travellers, men with beery voices and large suitcases, stopped. People came north from places like Cleveland to make deals on finished steel over in Hamilton, and they made a few deals in the Grand Trunk area while they were at it. Now this whole area is a little quiet in the industrial sense, because there's so much emphasis on Hamilton and Toronto, the production routes are all different, the Lake Boats haven't been active for several decades. Industry goes to Toronto and New Jersey by train and overnight trailer. Farming is good, property is fairly high.

Property and farming didn't interest me very much in actual fact when I was 11½, but the Grand River sure did. The Grand was a sanctuary of riverside lodges, which we built under crowded trees, partridge, you could hear their whirring wings seconds before you stumbled into their particular little clearings. We didn't have rowboats and it was too shallow to fish very much from the shore, we fished from other points and from the bridges, or under the bridges, but we enjoyed the proximity of the water.

These lodges were part of a whole route that included the Brantford Road, the abandoned Lime Kiln halfway to Brantford, the MacFarlane Factory, way south of Victoria Park, where they made parts for cameras and we would sometimes rummage through the huge dump outside the factory gates, looking for odd things of value, God knows, only to us. We weren't poor, our parents had real cameras. My father had a beautiful old Rolleiflex and a Leica as well; my sister, who went out with a photographer for a while, had some sort of sophisticated Kodak, but, nevertheless, a winder was a real find, a lens frame could be traded for a comic book maybe, it was something to do.

It was in one of these lodges, there only were 2 or 3 of any substance, tree branches and bits of building material, that Carolyn Demeroff, who had long curly dark squeaky-clean hair and always got As, often ahead of me, I admit, first showed me her breasts. I say first because she did this several times. The first was at her suggestion. We were just sitting there and there was no one else around. We weren't even sharing a forbidden cigarette. We were just talking. Carolyn Demeroff didn't share forbidden cigarettes. Not to my knowledge. We had been talking about other kids in Grade 8. A class we were both soon about to vacate. Suzy Emerson had come up in the conversation on some account. Carolyn said, 'Susan wears tight sweaters.' Which was true, Suzy did.

I said, 'She's in bloom.' This was an arcane expression that had come into our Grade 8 class from somewhere. And Susan was, but of course Carolyn was too.

After I said that Suzy was in bloom, Carolyn paused for a second and there was a moment's silence. I thought she thought I had been rude. I was quite sweet on Carolyn Demeroff, but we hadn't talked much before this particular spring. Then she said, politely but bold as brass, 'Have you ever seen a girl's breasts?'

I said, 'No.' I hadn't. Actually I had. I had seen my sister's in the bath, but that's different, and I'd seen pictures.

This *was* different. Carolyn undid the buttons of the shirt she was wearing, a ruffled sort of white blouse, very modest, and pulled the white cotton material slowly over to one side at which point, before my astonished eyes, there was a strange, mysterious, sort of botanical, lovely white breast. It made a deep impression on me, but I didn't do anything. I just sat there, transfixed, with a very tight feeling in the pit of my stomach.

After this event, Bobby Kilmer said to me, 'How do you know she's got two? You only saw one.' And I got a big handful of wet leaves and shoved them down his shirt.

The lodges were the scenes of various events. Smoking, open (but not mutual) masturbation, who could shoot the farthest, that was a subject of great concern, slingshot manufacture (slingshots were forbidden, in my house at least), comic book trades. I made a very significant Batman trade, a missing num-

ber I wanted desperately, in return for some low-level Archie &
Jughead comics.

But in general the Grand River was more a set of specific
places, objectives, a peacefulness, for me at that age, than it
was a river of mystery or adventure. I wasn't, in short, all that
concerned as to where it went after it flowed south of Galt.

We would come down the Cedar Creek Road on our bikes, CCMs and Raleighs, whooping and shouting like Indians; or maybe we were supposed to be cowboys. I'm not sure. I think it varied. Peter sometimes referred to himself as Red Cloud. We were 11 and 12. Bobby sometimes called himself Creek Deer. Billy was Wyatt Earp. Pronounced Wwaat. The Indians who lived in Southwestern Ontario were Hurons. Red Cloud and Creek Deer were Sioux Indians. But we felt the Sioux had lived just south of where we were. Whatever. I was Sitting Bull. Another Sioux. My hair was long that summer and one day my sister braided it for me at the back.

The Cedar Creek Road rolls west out of Galt and turned, in those days at least, into an amazing highway of important stops. We gave them the names of historic places. There was the Rutherford Quarry. Which we called Dry Run. It was a wet quarry, abandoned and filled in with water, a natural swimming place. Peter and I weren't allowed to swim there. A boy had drowned at Dry Run a couple of summers ago. His name was Mark. 'Mark Twain,' Peter used to say as we went past. Because we knew what the words Mark Twain meant. They meant the lead weight that a Mississippi riverboat pilot would drop on a cord to test the depth of the river. So there was an aura about the place and some limitation. Because of our parents. But we would get off our bikes and smoke a shared cigarette, sitting up on the rocks, and watch the older kids swim. There were girls in bathing suits. It was a good place. There was an abandoned truck stop past there which a lot of people, farm kids, I guess, mostly, used for a shooting range.

.22s. We used to get off our bikes and scour the range for used bullets, lead slugs, and copper casings. They were both worth picking up.

Then there was the frog pond. It was a large swampy pond just off the highway and down the hill from a large residential farm. They didn't have crops of any kind. The pond had a lot of frogs. We shot them quite callously with air rifles. After we got our air rifles, that is. We even had a frogs' legs supper one afternoon. Peter said Wyatt Earp didn't eat frogs' legs, but he was overruled. We fried them up over a small fire in a little frying pan we brought from home. Nobody came and chased us away. The people who owned the farm spent weeks at a time somewhere else. As far as we knew we were free to use their land as much as we wanted to until they came back.

A little farther on, and best of all in some ways, was the Red Maple Dog Kennels. They had spaniels, German shepherds, and greyhounds. The spaniels and shepherds were cute puppies, but the adult greyhounds were the most beautiful. There was something extraordinarily quick and alert about the greyhounds. They were shadowy. They could change direction in a flash. They were very muscular and deep-chested. They were almost like ghosts.

GALT FARMER'S MARKET
AND BEATTIE STREET HANGOUTS

Saturday mornings were always sunny and I would always go to the Galt Farmer's Market with my family. That is, my mother, or my mother and my sister. Sometimes my stepfather would come along and chew the fat with one or two of the farmers he knew from his truck business. My stepfather, who drank quite a lot on Friday evenings, quite frequently didn't get up until hours after we came home. But whoever was going, we would have breakfast by 8 o'clock and stroll marketwards by 9 at the latest.

I was always fascinated by the range of produce at the Market. I guess boys eat a lot at that age. Preparing the body for future trials. Most of the booths had chickens, ham, pig products, fruit and vegetables in the summer, eggs, fresh country breads, home preserves, ranging from jams to pickled cauliflower, fish in the summer, spread out on trays of ice-chips; occasionally there'd be a beef farmer with 1 or 2 sides of beef and they'd calmly saw off a freezer section while making a little conversation about the weather.

There were other displays. Baked goods, for example, not just the breads, but sweet things, pies, tarts, even chocolate layer cakes, sometimes with a jam filling. I used to get 50¢ a week allowance in those days. A drop in the bucket compared to the '80s, but it covered a variety of things, basics, necessities like films or bits for my chemistry set. This allowance was for my modest household chores, taking out ashes from the furnace, weeding our big vegetable garden in the summer. 50¢ wasn't all that much, but if I loafed around the bakery stalls long enough while my mother and sister were over on the other side, discussing ham and potatoes questions, I could usually find someone who needed a little help carrying some heavy bags to their car, or the Beattie Street bus stop. Sometimes this endeavour would yield a nickel, not enough for a tart, tarts were usually 10¢, but on other occasions the reward might be 25¢. Big time. I was becoming a capitalist. A little services-entrepreneur.

The Galt Farmer's Market was on Beattie Street. Scottish originally. You can usually tell by the 'ie' ending. And this was a good centre, like the centre of a brick house or, I used to imagine at times, a military square, c/w with its outdoor covered areas and parked trucks, '50s Fords and Chevs, a few Amish buggies, although the Amish stopped coming to Galt after a while because they found they could sell all their delicious goods each week over in Kitchener-Waterloo. 'That was where Napoleon met his Waterloo,' my sister said. And I guess she was right. Galt is in Wellington County. The Duke of Waterloo used German troops˙ along with the poor English guys. Napoleon wasn't all that popular outside of France. But I always liked the French as a child. I think I liked the French because I had read *The Hunchback of Notre Dame* as a child and thought that Paris sounded like a city of stirring adventures.

The weathered granite stone Town Hall was immediately above the Market. The Galt Police Department, c/w its 4-cell jail, was in the basement. 'Nice and cool in the summer,' Rex Willis was reputed to claim. He was in the slammer about once a month. And Tom Ridley's furniture store where I used to go with my stepfather and play with the old man's refinishing tools, while my stepfather talked up and away about the best way to make a lot of money repairing or perhaps redesigning people's back porches. 'Do the front porches,' said Ridley.

He was a perfectionist. He produced things of real beauty in that turpy varnish-scented old store, shavings scattered this way and that, on the south side of Main Street Creek. The Creek was just a trickle under the road, but you could see it between buildings on the south side. Ridley did cabinets with fine carving along the edges, bevelled glass, bird's-eye maple, like my sister Nancy's bedroom suite, great brass claw or embossed head handles. He showed me how to plane boards in the set-up on his big table vise. 'Do front porches,' he told my stepfather, glum in his big K-W gumboots. My stepfather was Irish, a lapsed Catholic and frequently morose. 'No, no,' he told Ridley, 'there's far too much work on a front porch, and besides they don't want it done.' I used to imitate him at times. He was friendly enough. But it was Ridley, with his gleaming cabinets, piles of fresh sawdust, delicate but much-handled tools, strong odorous varnishes, and neat brass locks & catches, who captivated my imagination.

Somehow or other I went to the movies about 3 times a week. I went Friday evening with my family, Saturday afternoon with Peter and Harold, and then if possible again on Saturday night, often by myself.

There were 3 cinemas in Galt and 2 of them, the Grand and the Capital, showed a different film on Saturday afternoons anyway.

Saturday afternoons were fun, but I went mostly in the summers. It was hot outside, sometimes so hot that the dogs were open tongue huffing in the street. The Grand and the Capital were air-conditioned and they abounded in cowboy films and Flash Gordon serials.

We would sit in a group on Saturday afternoons, there were always kids from my class at St. Andrew's, and stuff ourselves with popcorn while the tall men of the law chased short unshaven villains, bank robbers, or molesters of virtue out of Hanging Dog saloons through swinging doors and into the dusty streets of Dodge and Tucson. We never saw the foothills of Alberta or the famous shoot-outs of Timmins or Thunder Bay, but this wasn't Al Capone or Bugsy Siegel material either. These were stylized North American pastorals. The clothes, the affected way of speech, the guns, men in groups, farmers in shirtsleeves and suspenders, the open range, these were cattle films, cowpuncher epics. They were good on a hot afternoon.

I would probably be home for about 4 hours and then I would be out again. Galt was very peaceful. Nobody ever bothered me about going out by myself on a Saturday night.

Friday evenings we would go to see films like *Pinky, Harvey,*

The Birth of a Baby, which my mother took me to see as a part of improving my general education.

Saturday evenings I often went by myself. I saw *The Golden Horde* at the Palace on Main Street, *The Black Rose,* which I think was about Marco Polo and the archers of Ghenghis Khan, *The Lives of a Bengal Lancer,* one of my favourites, and *The Kid from Texas,* which made a great impression on me because of the green leather windbreaker that Audie Murphy wore in the film.

A film that still comes around that I saw by myself on one of those Saturday nights was *Five Fingers,* in which James Mason, of the deep, fruity voice, plays an embassy clerk shuttling between the British and the Germans, playing both sides, until he gets caught. I forget if they execute him or not, but there was a lovely scene in which Mason, whose code name is Cicero, talks about seeing a couple having dinner on a terrace, somewhere in South America, he sees this from the boat he's on, the couple have tall champagne glasses and the man has a white sports jacket. James Mason swears to himself that somehow or other he'll make enough money to become that man. This affected me very strongly. I still remember a certain thrill of excitement, as in entering a new room.

Friday and Saturday nights were different.

After seeing a film like *Pinky* with my mother and stepfather, in which a young black woman returns to the South after attending university up north, we would go across the street to George's, a Canadian/Chinese restaurant on south Water Street, and I would have my favourite order: toasted ham & lettuce, or ham & tomato on brown, with a chocolate milkshake.

But on Saturdays I would get out of the film in question around 9 and go for one of my walks: up Main Street to Moffat's restaurant, where next door there was a poolroom and bowling alley called Taylor's.

There at Taylor's I would install myself with a Coke and

watch the older boys play pool. This was a different kind of film. They were older. Some of them had cars. They talked about driving to Hamilton. One guy called Butch had been to a place called Calgary.

I would stay for about an hour, not too long, while they socked the coloured balls around and talked about basketball games and girls in high school. Then I would head home thinking about cars and girls and basketball. I was getting older. I couldn't wait to be in high school. High school was going to be glamorous. I already felt much older than most of my friends in Grade 8.

We lived in a large rambling gabled dusty red-brick house, and that was the name of one of our dogs, Dusty, a black chow, with huge smoky eyes and a purple tongue. With a hunter-green front porch that didn't need repairing or redesigning – yet – next to St. Andrew's School where I was a genius but incapable, absolutely, bewilderingly incapable of doing homework. This was just up the hill, Victoria Hill, from the Kenneth Hay Knife Co. Ltd., on the west side of Galt and very pleasant. But Victoria Hill wasn't as ritzy or as El Dorado as Blair Road where my grandfather, Duncan, lived in a comfortable apartment with his accumulation of prints, engravings, and etchings. 'Let me see your etchings,' I said to my sister, she was older, by six years, 'and I will tell you what kind of education you have had.' Cheeky. His service revolvers, dog-skull ashtrays, he smoked a pipe and occasionally a cigar. My father had never smoked or drunk, but Duncan, still lean and brown at 71, like a fish leaping in the Grand River, drank champagne by himself on Saturdays, my mother said it was a ritual, like those blue & yellow occult eye and star-embroidered leather Dutch Maid Cleanser aprons that men in their 50s wore at their strange meetings in the Masons. My sister, who loved Duncan wildly, said that Duncan was eccentric.

Blair Road was named after Blair in Scotland and the Lairds lived a couple of blocks past my grandfather's apartment building. They had an enormous house with a black iron fence and a Rolls-Royce parked in the gravel driveway. Old Broderick Laird had made his money in copper industrial fittings, and they obviously had pots of it. I would skim past on my blue CCM on my way to Duncan's, running an errand, some porkchops from Anderson & Stuart's, or taking the long way around through Blair to my friend Jaime's house, and I would see the huge gleaming silver insect of the Rolls and expect for some reason to see copper industrial fittings scattered over the infinite and immaculately kept golf-course of a green lawn. Greener than a billiards table.

Sometimes during that summer I would see Penny Laird sunbathing off to the side of the house as I took the corner of Maitland and Blair, a small side-street running north into a cul-de-sac and green trees 4 blocks on the other side of which Jaime lived in a simpler house. A portage. Jaime's mother made superb rice pudding, browned on top, with flat raisins.

Penny Laird was sixteen that summer and went to a private school where the girls wore uniforms, somewhere east of Hamilton. East of Hamilton was a mystery. She was one of those very beautiful blonde snub-nosed girls who probably dream of red cocker spaniels and always have exactly the right things to say in social situations – like the time I rode past and they were having an enormous garden party out on the front lawn. My sister and I had a circus at the side of our house one weekend and it involved a soap-box derby. and other children rolling down our terrace wrapped in sheets, but this was different. My sister knew Penny Laird's older brother, Harris, slightly. Harris was 20 and at university in Toronto and wore argyle socks and drank and played cards. There were rumours that he would not be coming back to Galt. My mother said they were probably going to pay him to go away somewhere. I pictured him beside the sea, Cornwall, perhaps, which I had read about, in a striped lawn-chair. Drunk, presumably.

I saw her sunbathing at least 2 or 3 times that summer. This was the summer that I began to appreciate thighs and toes and the gleam in people's hair. She was bronzed. Kids my age didn't suntan we just played outdoors. Penny Laird. Boy. She was recently back from Switzerland the time in particular that I saw her breasts and they were milky white like perfect globes or the headlights of the big Rolls parked in the gravel driveway.

She was lying on her stomach reading a book as I went past onto Maitland and I paused sitting there on my blue CCM under a big oak tree. Then while I was sitting there, just like magic, she rolled over calmly on one side to get another magazine. I presumed they were fashion magazines, but for all I know they were possibly *Time* or *Newsweek*. Those were the magazines my grandfather read. Just for a moment she was naked from the waist up, cool bronzed skin, white strap marks across her tan shoulders and those ultimate breasts like perfect baseballs. Then she straightened her slipped top, just a wisp of red-dotted dark blue silk, and stretched out again, dark magenta-framed glasses and a bottle of ginger ale.

Then I was gone, up on my pedals like a swallow. She didn't know my sister, although they were about the same age, but I didn't want to take any chances on someone hearing a story about my spying on the Lairds' green lawns or on Penny Laird while she sun-tanned and romped with her vicarious feather-footed cocker spaniels.

You can't tell. A chauffeur might have come out and asked me what I was doing. The servants probably thought their employers owned Maitland Street as well as the lovely house.

I rode into the cul-de-sac at the end of Maitland and the dark maple trees, uncomfortable on the hard black seat. I was wondering if I should tell Jaime about this experience, and if I should dress it up: Ah yes, she was naked, bronzed, just like a movie star, and there were two men with her, both of them wearing tuxedos with rings in their ears, or if I should just give him a friendly hint. I would never meet her. I saw a picture of her in a magazine years later but she was living in Montreal. I met her brother when I was in my 20s in Toronto, but he didn't have very much to say for himself, one way or the other. There were no copper industrial fittings scattered on the huge lawn after all. No clues as to how the old man made his money, or whether it was true that he drank brandy with his breakfast in the morning. It was like a picture from a magazine. The ginger ale in the bottle she had her slim hand around probably wasn't nearly as cold as it looked to me, sitting on the bike.

A large part of being 12 lies in the tension that exists between the strait-laced, stiff, dutiful sense of obligation demanded by school, MacIlwraith's history lessons, my competitions with Mark Filser, and, in my case, church — every Sunday morning at the great, weathered stone building on Grand Street, looking out toward the river, not called First Presbyterian Church, as in other SW Ontario towns, but, in this case, Knox's Church, so it was emphatic. Anyway, a large part of being 12 lies in the tension between these forms of deportment and the sheer ecstatic pleasure of unlimited excess.

One thing I was inordinately fond of at that age, and still am, for that matter, was peaches. August, late summer, when the evening light over the Grand River is starting to darken just a little earlier than it was in July, is the best month for peaches. You don't have to go to the supermarket to get the fancy grade-A tawny yellow with a faint rose blush peaches that have been getting better and better since July. There are always peaches on people's trees. Perhaps the Niagara version *is* a shade better. To some connoisseur intent on the finest extra taste of peach pit arsenic, that might be a little more marked in the Niagara version for some reason or another. But Galt isn't very far from the Niagara peninsula. Various people, not us, despite the size of our yard, had peach trees. One such peach tree, easily accessible, in the area of Victoria Hill where I lived at this time, was the Larkins'. Actually the Larkins had two peach trees. And they were lush and healthy.

Stealing these peaches was exciting. Of course, there is a profound moral reconsideration as you get older. You think back and remember one of these excursions with a vague sense of guilt. You think of the family getting up the next morning and glancing out into the backyard, not noticing anything different at first, just a few robins and sparrows playing back there, all the trees in order, lots of petunias and geraniums sitting happily in their black earth beds. Then all of a sudden like a deep significant forgotten thought they notice an absence of peaches, not really an absence so much as a particular area where there should be but don't seem to be any peaches at all. They go out on the back porch and study this phenomenal aberration. Jesus, they say, there aren't any peaches on that tree at all. Well there sure were yesterday. Then it slowly dawns on them, the Larkins, say, a nice couple, English – he worked as an engineer in the local foundry – that, God, somebody has come in and stolen all their peaches. Yesterday they were peachful, today they are peachless.

But that didn't bother us at the time. In fact it added to the general excitement and pleasure. We were indeed quite conscious that these people, and it wasn't just the Larkins, it was almost anyone in Galt who had a good peach crop during August, would get up the next morning and be surprised out of their socks.

'Surprised out of his shoes,' said Bobby.

'Surprised out of her panties,' said Alvin.

'Surprised out of her corsets,' giggled Sharon. Sharon only went with us about once on these raids, but she deserves to be mentioned. We would have contests to outdo each other in describing just how surprised these people would be when they woke up. We were heartless.

But we didn't think of these midnight peach raids, which involved slipping out of our 2nd floor bedroom windows after lights out, as genuine thefts. They weren't thefts in the same classification as Bobby's theft of Don Clark's new bicycle seat, for example. The bicycle seat theft, about a year ago, complete with a gorgeous zebra-skin cover, was thought of as a serious act. Not only did Bobby sweat out the moral seriousness of this theft after committing it, stealing it right off Clark's bike parked outside the library, where I used to read on Saturday afternoons sometimes instead of going to the current Green Hornet serial, not only did Bobby sweat this out in terms of how would he feel if sometime somebody – Clark, say – were to do this to him, he also made the mistake of telling his older brother. His older brother thought it was definitely a serious act. Among Protestants, I think, this distinction is vaguely comparable to mortal and venial sins. A theft is serious. So Bobby, as I remember, sweated even more. Then he simply returned the zebra-covered seat. He never did tell Clark that he'd taken it. It was a mystery for several weeks. Other kids in our Grade 7 would bring it up. Well, I wonder who did take Donny's zebra-covered bicycle seat? Maybe it was that guy with a store on Main Street who always drops in to the library to take out the art books. Maybe it was somebody from another town. Bobby never did clear it up. The point is he sweated, and the next point is he returned it, in perfect order.

The idea of the peaches, which we noticed on our way past the Larkins', or the Rankins', that was another excellent backyard, as a form of property in the same sense that Donny's bicycle seat was a form of property, never really occurred to us. On one hand, peaches on a tree were a form of nature, therefore they weren't really property. On the other hand, they were something an adult had left out of doors – 'Yeah,' said Gene, 'like a car or a motorcycle,' and we all laughed – and therefore they were more or less fair game.

Real thefts did take place occasionally. Not among us, we were too young and innocent, too dimpled, too in love with rafts, partridges, bicycles and snowball fights. But among some of the older boys the 'game' was a bit more serious. Industrial equipment always fascinated me as a child, and still does, for that matter; but we never stole anything serious or industrial at that time, because it wasn't part of nature. 'Of course,' said

Gene, who was something of a philosopher at that age, 'what would the situation be if, say, you went and stole somebody's dog? That'd be different, right?' But we all had dogs. 'Yeah, but suppose you went and stole Tommy Henderson's dog, that big Irish setter? That would be a serious crime, that would be actual theft.' Gene was probably right. The older boys, whatever else they did, didn't steal dogs. They didn't steal from other boys. Or from younger boys. They stole from stores, or from factories. Wrenches from service stations, knife sets from the Kenneth Hay Knife Co. Ltd., batteries from parked cars. Even cars occasionally. But naturally, these were always returned.

And so every August, still lots of time before school, the great peach thefts. Usually around one or so in the morning. Dark. Except for later in August when our raids took place under a growing moon, once in a while a raid under a full moon. The night Carolyn Demeroff came with us in Grade 8, except that we weren't really in Grade 8 anymore, we'd graduated, we weren't even in public school anymore – we were big, and her Hawaiian sport shirt came undone as we were sliding down the Ferris's tree over on Robinson Street. That was under a full moon. And so I remember it distinctly. 'O hell,' she said, and she put her peaches in the brown paper bag she'd brought, a big one, before she bothered doing up her shirt.

After the theft, we would find a secluded spot a few blocks away, make ourselves comfortable, and begin slowly devouring the peaches. Not all of them, but a good number. The rest would be taken home, put carefully away in our rooms, and then eaten the next day, usually at school or after school. Stolen peaches, fresh from the tree, juicy enough to drip down your chin, do have a special taste. But the planning, the anticipation, the group structure c/w all its necessary secrecy and passwords and philosophical gambits, the darkness, the adventure of as common a thing as entering other people's backyards in the dark of night while they are innocently sound asleep was what made it exciting. Or the night Carolyn's shirt came undone, the night Gene stumbled over a lawn-mower that the Dellers' idiot child had left directly under the wire fence behind the stucco house, and yelled at the top of his voice, 'Jesus Christ, I've cut my leg,' or the night Bobby was throwing bits of wood up into the Larkins' tree and a badly aimed piece went flying up against a bedroom window of the house next door, presided over by an ugly couple, who sat out in their backyard a lot during the summer, and we all fled, instantly. These were the elements that made the great peach thefts more than a good idea, or a passing fancy, or an opportunity to see Carolyn's breasts. They made them a luminous, but innocent adventure. It was a test of our strength against adults. Although if we were caught, it was nothing more serious than peaches.

Every chestnut-scented scuffed running-shoe fall in Galt, after Labour Day and school had begun again, the Galt Fair was the major event in town before Thanksgiving. Even the year, 1950, that the Goldie-McCullough workers went on strike, the Fair was still, for most of us, even kids like Gene and myself who went down to watch the workers on picket, far and away the biggest event in town. It was what people talked about, in addition to school, sports, could the Tigers defeat the Yankees or couldn't they, could the Habs beat the Leafs, it was about time, and, of course, escapades.

The Galt Fair wasn't a huge complex event like the Chicago World's Fair, for example, but it was exciting. First of all they had an excellent side-show. The Bearded Woman, the Man with No Arms. The baseball and wheel of fortune games were good. There were a few rides, one Ferris wheel; but the emphasis was more on things you participated in. There was more apple pie than a troop of marines could have eaten. Second, everybody came to the Fair: families, kids from other schools, naturally, people I didn't know I was related to, store owners, bank tellers, policemen I recognized from the local stock-car races, just about everybody. They had quarter-horse races and I used to bet on these races with Bobby and Gene. I was lucky, and this used to mean more money to spend. More country hamburgers, side-shows, and tricky games of skill.

'How would you like to have your first sexual experience with someone like that?' Gene said as we came out of the Bearded Woman's tent. She was definitely a woman, there was no mistake about that, dressed in a pink corset with yellow ribbons in her dark curly hair. And bearded. The question, I guess, was, Is the beard real? And we had decided it must be, because several people were invited to come up from the audience and examine it. 'Abnormal *genes,*' said Bobby. Gene hit him. 'I've already had my first sexual experience,' I told them both, lying, not lying just boasting. 'Pillows don't count,' said Gene, 'and Carolyn Demeroff likes Peter Morris better than she likes you.' This was cruel of Gene, it was below the belt, but partially true, I suspected.

'Maybe the midget does it with her,' said Gene. He was very serious about this particular show, very curious about the bearded woman. We had been to see the midget, actually he was a good 3 feet tall, and very well-dressed, tuxedo, spats, white evening scarf, despite the fact that it was a warm fall night.

We had been on the Ferris wheel twice and were bored with rides anyway. There were boxing matches at the Fair, and we would cheer wildly for whichever thick-eared local youth, probably from nearby Hamilton. 'Pugs,' my sister called them derisively, or, worse, 'factory boys.' I had the impression that this was not my preferred path in life. But I thought about it. It seemed to me that it would take years, well of course it would, before I would ever be that deep-chested or have such muscular arms. 'They don't make any money,' said Bobby, 'they just fight in fairs. If you want to make money you have to be black like Joe Louis.' I had a framed photograph of Joe Louis, the Brown Bomber. It was one of my favourite possessions. Not part of a series like my baseball card collection, but it was a real photograph, nicely framed. It was a lot classier than a piece of cardboard with Ted Williams' RBIs printed out on the back.

The Strongest Man in the World was always a disappointment. He didn't do anything except lift weights, and we swore it was rigged. The weights were heavy though. Various townspeople would go up on stage at the Barker's invitation and have a heft to no avail.

There were shooting galleries, innumerable board games, wheel of fortune games, no cash, of course, just kewpie dolls, pandas, bracelets to give your sister (I would give mine to Carolyn Demeroff), knock down the wooden bottles with a baseball games. I was good at knocking down the wooden bottles, but Gene was the best rifle shot.

Fatima was something special. You had to be 18 to get into that show, in a large striped tent from which issued sinuous strains of presumably Eastern music. But we tried peeking under the tent, it seemed logical, but it was pegged down as tight as a box lid. Once we did discover a small split in the canvas, but even then we couldn't see very clearly. It was exciting, but we didn't see anything very graphic.

The Fair lasted for five days. That included all the stock-judging events, a special performance by the high school marching band, a beauty contest, the works.

'So what do we want to do next?' Bobby asked. He was talking to me more than to Gene. He was ticked off with Gene for refusing to loan him some extra money. This wasn't my fault. There hadn't been any quarter-horse betting this evening.

'We should go and watch the stock-judging,' said Gene very airily, 'at least you learn something from stuff like that.'

'Why, are you going to be a farmer when you grow up?'

'Suck,' said Gene, 'I *am* grown up.'

We thought we were.

But we got derailed from the stock-judging event because we ran into Brad Simmons and went to see the Siamese Twins with him. His sister, whom Gene had been a little sweet on at one point, had opted out. She'd seen it the year before and gave us her comments before we headed over.

'It's icky,' she said, 'you should come on the Ferris wheel.'

The Siamese Twins was the show the girls seemed to like the best, however. They liked giggling over it, and they liked being horrified. They would gasp with horror as the Barker went over the life history and different attributes of the Twins, a boy and a girl, joined at the hip and the head. The boys, for some reason, thought this one was just dumb. But once again, Gene seemed interested.

After the Siamese Twins, we saw an American pilot who had been shot down over North Korea the previous year. He came out in full pilot's gear, sheepskin-lined jacket, goggles loose around his neck, quite a nice-looking guy, and talked about his experiences for a while and then answered questions. The audience would ask him stuff like, 'When are we going to win this war?' And he would say, 'Soon. It's almost over. In fact, it could be over right while we're standing here.' Or somebody would ask him, 'Why are we over there fighting those people?' And he was usually a bit slow on this one. One night Jack Tucker, who was an older guy and a notorious drinker, yelled out, 'When you get yourselves fully trained after Korea, you should come up here and try us out.'

'We'd beat them easy,' said Gene, 'we've got precision pilots, they've just got guys who go out on luck.'

'A wing and a prayer,' I said. I was beginning to think about Brad Simmons' sister and the Ferris wheel.

'Yeah, like Roy Campanella,' said Bobby, he was a big Campanella fan. 'I'll bet,' he said, swallowing the last of his 5th hot dog and throwing the napkin in front of a fat woman towing 2 little girls with red braids.

Then there were card tricks, stealing other kids' hats, splashing girls with lemonade or Coke, always a stray puppy who had wandered into the side-show area from somone's tent or maybe from the cattle area, and, of course, standing around swapping stories with other kids from school.

There was a great booth that last fall. It hadn't been there in previous years. There was a woman who was billed as Wanda the Amazon. She was very tall and aristocratic. She must have been at least 6'4" or even taller. And she was quite well-built, no two ways about that. Gene liked her a great deal, he went about 5 times. It became a joke. 'Hey, Gene,' Bobby would say, 'are you and Wanda going steady?'

She was probably from some place like Michigan, but she was billed as having been born in the steamy Amazon jungle, had taught archery and spear-throwing as a child, and had been brought to North America in captivity. I don't know how they explained that legally, if anyone asked, but here she was performing at local fairs for our edification.

I watched her once, and then I went back a second time with Gene. Bobby was busy knocking down wooden milk bottles. She was amazingly beautiful. Tall, lightly muscled, but she looked as if she could pick up a small steer and toss it around. The Barker said she had done things like that before she was brought to North America. He had a lot of things to say about the mysterious tribe she was supposed to have come from, but it sounded like bull. She herself was terrific. We watched her shoot apples suspended in front of a target with a bow and arrows. She wasn't a better shot than we were, she was better than Bobby, but she wasn't better than Gene or myself who were products of summer playground archery practice, but she was definitely more impressive. She had a sort of short leopard-skin tunic and green paint on her toenails. Long dark hair, young; great jugs, as Bobby had observed. She was terrific. Then an assistant set up a small cotton sheep, and Wanda speared it from 30 or 40 feet. Effortlessly. 6'4". What more does it take to be an Amazon? Gene was hooked. I think he was in love with her. Wham. From Joe DiMaggio to Wanda the Amazon in one visit.

Gene got her autograph before we left. He said she smelled of musk. Then he said no, it was violets. We hooked up with Bobby who had borrowed some money from his brother, and then we went over to the stock-judging event. Prize bulls, prize cows, Angus, Herefords, Holsteins, Guernseys.

The horses would be the following night. And then in another day or two, I would be off to Toronto. A new school, a new district, new friends. I gave Bobby my entire comic book collection. Gene was killed 2 years later in a motor-boat accident on Lake Huron.

ACKNOWLEDGMENTS

Some of these poems and prose pieces have appeared previously, in the same or different versions: 'Chocolate,' 'Rowing,' and 'Eastman Kodak' in *The Malahat Review*; 'Hills' and 'Dancing at the Renovated King Edward (VII)' in *Exile*; 'Stamp Collecting' appeared in the author's first book *The Blue Sky*. The stories 'Late Summer Dinners' and 'Fishing' were first published in *The Malahat Review*, and parts of '24th of May,' 'Grand River,' 'The Fabulous Lairds,' and 'The Great Peach Thefts' were broadcast on CBC's State of the Arts.

•

The author would like to thank the Canada Council and the Ontario Arts Council for their financial assistance during the gestation and writing period of this book. He would also like to thank various persons: Barry Callaghan, Geoff Hancock, Constance Rooke, and Linda Spalding for their encouragement; Russell Brown for his considerable patience with the early versions of this work; and Katherine Ashenburg of the CBC for her suggestions on some of the stories in 'Light Photographs.' Even finished manuscripts don't make books. The author would also like to thank Bernice Eisenstein for her scrupulous checks on everything from capitals to the origins of chocolate. Finally, he would like to thank Ellen Seligman for her resourcefulness and general suggestions on order.